Towards a
New Theory of
Distributive
Justice

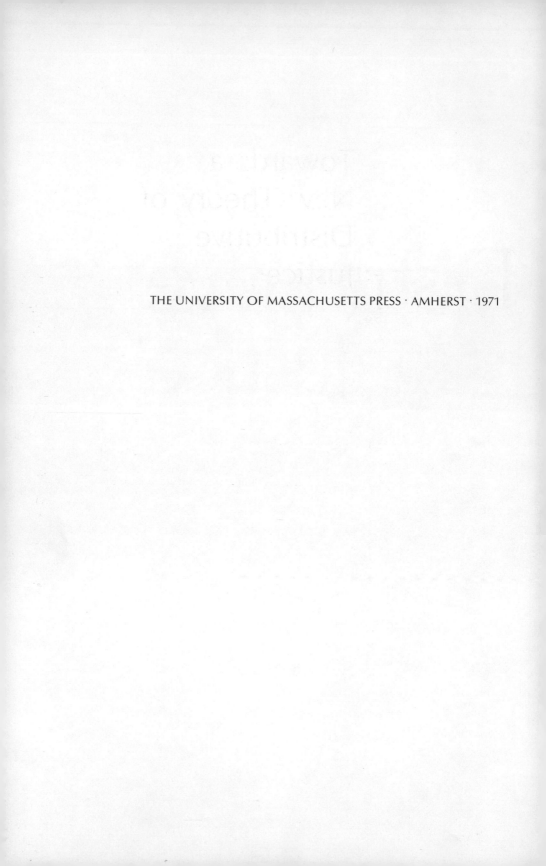

THE UNIVERSITY OF MASSACHUSETTS PRESS · AMHERST · 1971

Towards a

New Theory of

Distributive
Justice

Norman E. Bowie

To Bonnie

Preface

THIS BOOK is the end product of a project I began in 1967 as a doctoral candidate at the University of Rochester. I am greatly indebted to a number of teachers and colleagues whose criticism and encouragement have provided the motivation for completing this task. I also owe a special debt to a number of authors since their ideas have stimulated my own. It is impossible to recall everyone who has influenced me, but some deserve acknowledgement here.

My dissertation advisor, Professor Richard Taylor, saw the project through its early stages and always had that word of encouragement when my spirits were low. Three other professors at the University of Rochester were invaluable at this time. Professor Theodore Bluhm first aroused my interest in political philosophy and made many helpful suggestions in that area. Professor Robert Holmes provided careful scrutiny of the manuscript and enabled me to avoid a number of errors. Finally, I am indebted to Professor Colin Turbayne who introduced me to the language model and showed me its heuristic potential. I have applied a technique which he has used successfully in his own work. See Colin Murray Turbayne, *The Myth of Metaphor* (New Haven: Yale University Press, 1962) revised edition (Columbia: University of South Carolina Press, 1970).

Research for this book led me into philosophy, political science, and economics, and I have drawn from and been influenced by many in these areas. Footnote references do not do justice to the influence of some authors, however. Professor Nicholas Rescher's book *Distributive Justice* is the starting point for any discussion in this area. My own chapter on utilitarianism is in many ways an elaboration of his own strategy in criticizing utilitarianism. My discussion of economic utilitarianism is also quite explicitly influenced by I. M. D. Little's *Welfare Economics*. I should also state that I have accepted two of Professor Rescher's conclusions: (a) that distributive justice is a function of the economic status of a society and (b) that the problem of distributive justice is best viewed as a conflict of competing claims (values).

What I have done is to try to specify how the conflicts can be resolved using on the one hand a detailed classification of societies and actual principles of distributive justice on the other. A much abbreviated discussion of Chapter III appears in my article, "Equality and Distributive Justice" which appeared in *Philosophy* (April 1970). I appreciate the permission of the editors of *Philosophy* to incorporate that article in this work.

My analysis of the concept of need is influenced by S. I. Benn and R. S. Peters's discussion in *The Principles of Political Thought*. Finally, I have been influenced by the series of articles on justice of Professor John Rawls. Like Professor Rescher, Rawls sees the problem as one of competing values; however, he chooses to resolve the conflict by a procedural method.

I should like to thank colleagues and friends for commenting upon various sections of revisions of the manuscript. My Hamilton colleagues, Elizabeth Ring, Robert Simon, and especially Russell Blackwood, have been invaluable. I should also like to express appreciation to Rex Martin of the University of Kansas and special thanks to my friend and advisor on economics, Douglas Dobson.

Financial support for my dissertation was provided by an NDEA fellowship and by the University of Rochester. Additional support in the revision of the manuscript was supplied by Hamilton College.

Finally, I should like to recognize the influence of two undergraduate Bates College professors, Professor of Economics Ralph Chances and especially Professor of Philosophy Joseph D'Alfonso whose inspirational teaching and scholarship are responsible for my interest in economics and philosophy. I extend a special note of thanks to my wife Bonnie whose assistance and support have sustained me throughout.

The following publishers and editors have kindly permitted me to quote from the works mentioned: the editors of Nomos VI, "Constitutional Liberty and the Concept of Justice" by John Rawls, "Marx and Distributive Justice" by Robert C. Tucker; the editors of The Review of Economic Studies, "The General Theory of Second Best" by R. G. Lipsey and K. Lancaster; Macmillan Company, *Economics of Welfare* by Cecil Arthur Pigou, "Equality As a Social Objective" in *Politics and Economics* by Lionel Robbins, *The Methods of Ethics* by Henry Sidgwick; the Aristotelian Society, "Justice and Liberty" by D. D. Raphael; Cambridge University Press, *Principia Ethica* by G. E. Moore; the editors of *The Philosophical Review*, "Justice as Fairness" by John Rawls; Prentice Hall, Inc. "Justice and Equality" by Gregory Vlastos in Richard Brandt, Ed., *Social Justice*, © 1962; Russell & Russell, "The Constitutional Code" by Jeremy Bentham in *The Works of Jeremy Bentham* John Bowing, Ed., (1838–1843), © 1962; Yale University Press, *National Economic Policy* by James Tobin; Clarendon Press, *A Critique of Welfare Economics* by I. M. D. Little; The Royal Institute of Philosophy and the editor of *Philosophy* "Equality and

Equity" by D. D. Raphael; The Bobbs Merrill Company, Inc., *Distributive Justice* by Nicholas Rescher, copyright © 1966, *Utilitarianism* by John Stuart Mill, edited by Oskar Piest, copyright © 1957 by the Liberal Arts Press Inc.; The University of Chicago Press. *Capitalism and Freedom,* by Milton Friedman, copyright © 1962, *The Road To Serfdom* by Friedrich A. Hayek, copyright © 1944, Albert Fried and Ronald Sanders, eds., "Code of Nature" by Morelly, "Babeuf's Defense" by Gracchus Babeuf, and "What is Property" by Pierre Joseph Proudhon. All these articles were published in *Socialist Thought—A Documentary History.* (Garden City, N.Y.: Doubleday & Co., 1964) © 1964 by Albert Fried and Ronald Sanders.

NORMAN E. BOWIE
November 1970

Contents

.

Bowie: Distributive Justice

Introduction

NEITHER THE sophistication of science nor the current uncertainty about the nature and objectivity of values has appreciably diminished man's propensity to describe the actions, purposes, and characters of his fellow human beings as just or unjust. To assert that someone is unjust is to provide moral censure and to provoke the accused to defend himself. The quarreling husband and wife, the labor leader and the entrepreneur, the Republicans and the Democrats, and the opposing sides of a military dispute all provide elaborate cases to show that their cause is just and that of their opponents unjust.

The far-ranging scope of these disputes testifies to the importance of questions of justice. The unsettled and chaotic nature of these disputes testifies to the fact that there is no agreement as to the nature of justice nor any accepted formula for determining what is just and unjust. This inability to provide an acceptable account of justice and to determine in outline what is just and what is unjust constitutes the problem of justice.

Traditionally, the philosophers have tried to provide answers to the recurrent problem of justice. They have attempted both to define justice and to provide criteria for determining what is just. In the twentieth century, however, the problem of justice has not been a significant issue for philosophy in general or for moral philosophy in particular. This lack of interest probably results from the basic thrust of twentieth-century philosophy. The extreme empiricism, characteristic of both logical atomism and logical positivism, has influenced contemporary philosophy long after these schools passed from the scene. Philosophers have been interested in the facts, or more accurately, in the epistemological and logical problems of determining the facts. Logic, epistemology, and the philosophy of science provide the setting for the major contributions of twentieth-century philosophy. Metaphysics and value theory have not only declined in importance, but have found their very existence threatened. It has been fashionable to believe that ethical judgments or statements of value are noncognitive, unfalsifiable, and not amenable to the canons of deductive and inductive logic. Hence it has been thought that ethical disputes could not be resolved; if ethical terms had any meaning at all, they had emotive meaning only. They expressed the speaker's approval or disapproval.

The more recent shift of interest to language and "language games" mitigated this extreme empiricism to some extent. Description is not the only function of language. The descriptive function may very well be emphasized when considering the philosophy of science. However, an analysis of other uses of language may illuminate other philosophical problems. To rule out philosophical problems because they are not fully analyzable the way factual problems are borders on parochialism. Hence the scope of philosophy was broadened and analysis through ordinary language was held to be the key to the resolution of philosophical problems. Although admittedly broad in scope and fruitful in results, this approach has had little influence on social and political philosophy and very limited applicability to traditional problems of normative ethics. Many ethicists have "glossed over" this fact by insisting that the job of the philosopher is to analyze ethical terms, to distinguish ethical from nonethical terms, and to determine if and to what extent moral assertions can be proved. It has been assumed that these latter questions could be kept distinct from the so-called normative questions of right and wrong. The solution to normative questions was no longer considered to be the proper job of philosophers. Hence the problem of justice was implicitly no longer a bona fide philosophical issue.

Unlike other problems which have dropped out of philosophical discussion, the normative problem of justice has not been taken up by other disciplines. The reason for this is fairly clear. The problem of justice involves value judgments and is not simply a matter of describing the facts. A cultural anthropologist may describe what people believe to be just, but it is not considered an anthropological question to determine what *is* just. The same conclusion obtains when "economics," "psychology," and "political science" are substituted for "anthropology." So long as science is considered value-free, and as long as the disciplines cited above are concerned with their reputation as sciences, the normative problems of justice will lie outside these disciplines. Although each discipline does have its renegades, on the whole the philosophical problem of justice has not been incorporated into the network of issues in which social sciences are engaged.

From these considerations, the following conclusion seems appropriate: Although the public continues to use the concepts of justice and injustice and to debate about what is and what is not just, the normative problem of justice is no longer a serious object of scholarly investigation.

To a small extent, this book is a response to that conclusion. The book investigates the limited problem of distributive justice. I shall treat the question of distributive justice as a problem of moral philosophy in the traditional sense. I shall isolate the values to which one appeals when defending the assertion, "X is a just distribution." Often these values will be in conflict. Then I shall try to make a reasonable value judgment of my own; I shall try to determine what values are relevant to questions of distributive justice.

The purpose of Chapter I is to define carefully the problem, to pinpoint its scope, to indicate the limitations of my discussion, and to state clearly the assumptions upon which the book rests. It is to this task that I now turn.

I. The Problem of Distributive Justice Defined

Distributive and retributive justice. Traditionally, a distinction which goes back to Aristotle exists between distributive justice and retributive (corrective) justice. "Distributive justice" refers to the just distribution of benefits and burdens among a group of people. "Retributive justice" refers to the just administration of punishment. This book is concerned exclusively with distributive justice. It is confined in this way for the following reasons:

First, the basis for a just distribution of benefits and burdens is logically distinct from the basis for just punishment. This line of thought seems reasonable when one realizes that distributive and retributive justice arise from different situations. The need for retributive justice arises because men often break the laws or moral codes of the groups to which they belong. The need for distributive justice arises because men's wants and desires often exceed the means of fulfillment. This gap between desire and satisfaction results either from inadequate resources or from logically contradictory desires between two agents, X and Y, where X desires one thing and Y desires something incompatible with it, and only one person can be satisfied at that time and place. Hence, distributive justice provides the rules for the allocation of scarce resources and for the elimination of conflicting desires. Retributive justice provides the basis for punishment when such rules of distributive justice are violated. The tax policy a community uses may be based on distributive justice. The punishment for tax evasion may be based on retributive justice. It is important to keep these two issues distinct.

Secondly, the problem of retributive justice seems addressed to certain questions. For example, does the view that a criminal deserves punishment have connotations of simple revenge, and is the moral basis of punishment solely utilitarian? With distributive justice, there is no focus on certain questions, nor is there even a consistent division into opposing camps of opinion. Instead, thinking on distributive justice is schizophrenic, or to use the philosophical term, contradictory. At present, the conceptual issues are so confused that there are philosophical problems of analysis and clarification which must be solved before consistent positions on distributive justice can be formulated. Only then can the opposing positions be evaluated.

Finally, there is the practical problem; a comprehensive treatment of both retributive justice and distributive justice would simply be too involved. For these reasons I have decided to focus on distributive justice alone.

Distinctions. With respect to distributive justice, the following distinctions are important.

First, a distinction should be made between the production aspect and the distribution aspect of distributive justice. In philosophical discussion, there is a widespread tendency to take the supply of goods as given and to deal exclusively with problems of distribution. Thus justice is analyzed in a static system where the supply of what is to be allotted is constant. This position assumes that the supply of goods, 1, 2, 3, . . . n, is given. No account is taken of the production of these goods. Such an assumption vastly simplifies the problem, but unfortunately there remains a wide gap between the static theoretical results and the dynamic problems of distributive justice. Not only is one important aspect omitted from discussion, but remarks which are entirely appropriate in a static system may be completely inappropriate in a dynamic system. Furthermore, discussions of distributive justice of a non-philosophical nature emphasize the production aspect. This is especially true in economics. To consider the production aspect, one not only asks how we distribute a supply of commodities 1, 2, 3, . . . n, but also how any distribution will affect the quantity of the commodities produced, i.e., will n decrease or increase as the result of some distribution. For example, if the community were told that all goods would be distributed equally, this might so affect the incentive to produce, that there would be very few goods produced. Since questions of this type are important and widespread in the literature, I shall discuss the production aspect of distributive justice wherever such discussion seems appropriate. Hence, this book will attempt to consider distributive justice in its dynamic context, treating both the production of goods and their distribution.

Secondly, the problem of distributive justice can be viewed within various frameworks, some positive, some negative. Not only benefits, but also burdens, must be distributed. We can speak of distributing the vote, the profits of a company, or a new discovery in medicine. We can also speak of distributing the burdens of the draft, the drudgery of certain types of unpleasant work, or the nuisance of civic responsibilities. In general, problems of distributive justice arise either when our wants and desires surpass the available means of satisfaction or when unpleasant tasks must be done by some of the citizens but not by all. The emphasis of this book is on the first disjunct, on the distribution of benefits rather than on the distribution of burdens. However, the conclusions reached with respect to the first disjunct apply equally well to the second.

Even the discussion of the distribution of benefits has a positive and a negative side. One can emphasize the satisfaction of the benefits received or the dissatisfaction of the desires that remain unfulfilled. For example, suppose A and B each desire 10 units of commodities x, y, and z. This means there must be 20 units of x, y, and z available to satisfy the desires of both A and B. Since problems of distributive justice arise when there is a disparity between desires and goods, let us assume that the total available supply of x, y, and z is only 10 units each. Given that A and B both receive some of x, y, and z, we can speak of distributing the benefits x, y, and z, or we can speak of distributing the burden which results when neither A nor B are fully satisfied. I shall speak of distributing satisfaction rather than dissatisfaction.

Thirdly, the problem of distributive justice may have two starting points. (a) One can limit the discussion to a general theory of distribution, providing the general principles for a just production and distribution. With this starting point, the only data given are the resources available for production and some facts about the needs and desires of human beings. This approach assumes that as yet no benefits have been produced or distributed. This approach is not hopelessly unrealistic, however; it does apply to the real world. The general principles are constrained by the productive capacity of various societies and to some extent by the traits of human beings. However, this starting point is not limited simply to some particular distributive system. (b) One can begin with the *status quo*. This approach starts with certain productive and allocative patterns currently existing in some society. If one follows this approach, present distributions are evaluated and often suggestions are presented for alternative means of production and distribution. Obviously one cannot make this evaluative judgment unless one has some general principles of distributive justice against which the *status quo* can be evaluated. Hence the starting point of (b) is logically dependent on (a).

This book is limited to starting point (a). Suppose one should adopt starting point (b). In order to provide an adequate theory of distributive justice, he would have to consider the costs of redistribution. This factor of redistribution costs would greatly complicate an already complex analysis. Moreover, to begin with some particular distributive arrangement would limit the analysis to an undesirable extent. I prefer to begin with theoretical principles and then see to what extent they can be applied. Hence I will limit my discussion to (a) and proceed on the assumption that no production or distribution has taken place. An evaluation of present patterns of distribution and the costs of redistribution are discussions for someone else. For this reason I shall not be discussing directly current disputes about redistribution, i.e., I shall not be solving social problems. However, this discussion is clearly applicable to current patterns of distribution and is philosophically relevant to current social issues.

The problem. With this analysis before us, perhaps I can cite some problems of distributive justice and from these examples abstract in precise terms the problem which will occupy this book. Such problems include:

1. Who should receive a college education?
2. What are the considerations which constitute a just wage?
3. What standard of living, if any, should everyone be guaranteed?
4. What constitutes a fair price?

The purpose of this book is not to provide specific answers to these or similar questions; in fact, a philosopher could not give specific answers because such answers depend in part on complex factual considerations which lie beyond the philosopher's authority. Instead, the purpose is to examine the following question which can be abstracted from the four problems above and subjected to philosophical analysis. This abstract question can be formulated as follows:

Given: some society in which certain goods and services will be produced and distributed and in which it is impossible that there be enough to satisfy everyone's desire for them. On what basis or according to what principles can these goods and services be produced and distributed justly?

This is the question to which this book is addressed. It should be noted that both the production aspect and the actual distribution aspect are included. I have also stated the problem in positive terms and have omitted from consideration discussion of current patterns of distribution and the costs of redistribution when a current pattern falls below the standard. This is in accordance with the discussion above.

Prescription and description. I must make explicit to what extent this book is descriptive and to what extent it is prescriptive. With respect to the question of distributive justice, it is prescriptive. I am not concerned with the sociology of distributive justice, with the ways in which any society or all societies actually distribute goods and services. Instead I intend to provide an account of how goods and services ought to be distributed.

One qualification must be made immediately, however. I do feel constrained by our clearest and most basic notions about the nature of justice. If a theory sanctions as just any distribution which seems self-evidently unjust, then the theory is inadequate in that respect. In other words, an adequate theory of distributive justice must be free from obvious counterexamples.

In addition, the prescriptive account utilizes data of a descriptive or factual nature. As we shall see, disputes about justice result when values are in conflict. I shall accept as data those values which the antagonists recurrently cite to justify their claim that x is just or that x is unjust. For example, one often appeals to the value of equality as the basis for some distribution x. However, someone else quickly counters with an appeal to the value of happiness which is sacrificed by this distribution x. Such values as equality and happiness will be accepted as data.

Moreover, the prescriptive account will be constrained by facts about human nature, the state of technology, and the scarcity of goods and resources. An adequate account of distributive justice cannot be based on fictions that goods are plentiful, that men are without needs and desires, or that technology has reached some state which far exceeds today's. Although I shall offer a prescriptive account, it is an account which takes cognizance of the facts of the world in which we live.

However, the discussion of distribution will still be limited to moral concerns. I will not consider suggestions that the problem of distributive justice be solved by nonmoral means, e.g., by the might of the stronger, by coercion, or by cunning. I do not doubt that in many cases the problem could be solved or is solved in one of these ways. However, such a solution would not be a moral solution, and it is a moral solution to the problem of distribution which I seek.

Since the problem of distributive justice bridges a great many disciplines, especially economics, political science, and psychology, I must also make explicit my method for treating the relevant material from these other disciplines. A comprehensive philosophical treatment of the issues requires that some attention be given to the work performed in these disciplines. This is necessary because much of the nonphilosophical discussion is either explicitly or implicitly of great philosophical significance. This interlocking of disciplines presents a quandary, since comments on discussions which lie beyond my particular field of expertise must be made if the work is to be genuinely comprehensive. I have tried to resolve this quandary in the following manner:

Consideration of nonphilosophical disciplines is limited to a discussion of philosophical problems which arise from those disciplines and which are relevant to the overall philosophical problem. On occasion, empirical data from these disciplines will be relevant. Here my task is limited solely to an explanation of the relevance of the data to the philosophical problem. I shall not try to establish the truth or falsity of the empirical claims. For example, I shall argue that in some respects certain facts about human needs and capacities are relevant to questions of justice. Furthermore, I will accept the psychological claim that the satisfaction of certain desires is a necessary condition for the satisfaction of other desires. My purpose in citing these facts is to show the implication of this empirical claim for an adequate philosophical account of justice. I shall, however, offer no proof that we do in fact have such needs. My remarks on any empirical issue are always implicitly in the conditional form—if S is right in asserting X, then X has implication Y for the problem of distributive justice.

Assumptions. It is appropriate to state the assumptions operative throughout the book. First, I accept the fact that men have certain values which they seek to realize, that these values often come into conflict, and that such conflicts of value can produce moral problems. I assume that these problems are genuine moral problems, not pseudoproblems. Not only is our linguistic description of such problems meaningful, but moral assertions about these problems cannot be reduced or analyzed into some other nonmoral assertion without loss of meaning. Moral problems cannot simply be explained away.

Secondly, I assume that a worthwhile philosophical discussion of distributive justice can take place without a prior resolution of the higher-order questions of contemporary value theory. Such higher-order questions include the following:

1. Is the assertion that "x is valuable" subjective or objective?
2. What is a value? Does the word refer only to an external object, or to the psychological state of the agent, or to a relation between the agent and the external object?
3. What kind of property is the property of being valuable?
4. What are the necessary and sufficient conditions which distinguish a value from something else?

I do not omit such questions because I believe them to be unimportant. On the contrary, they are questions of great importance. Neither do I omit them because I believe them to be satisfactorily answered. In fact, they remain questions of such dispute that the controversy surrounding them has completely eclipsed other questions of moral philosophy. This book concentrates on one of these neglected areas and temporarily places the higher-order questions in philosophical limbo. If this is not done the discussion of distributive justice would never get started. I believe this move does not eliminate the possibility of a meaningful discussion of distributive justice.

The above finesse of higher-order questions requires a third assumption; a list of values must be compiled. It is assumed that these values are elements which one tries to achieve in just distribution. The list is comprehensive in the sense that it represents those values to which appeal is most often made in the literature. They are the basic constituents of the traditional theories and will be the basic constituents of my own theory as well. Hence this list of values plays a central role in what is to follow. The values will be roughly characterized in Chapter V for use in my own theory. With respect to other theories, the relevant values will be defined within each theory. The list includes the following:

1. happiness
2. liberty
3. equality
4. merit
5. optimization or efficiency
6. ability or skill.

Fourthly, I shall assume that whenever it is in one's power, one ought to do those acts which produce value and to avoid those acts which produce disvalue. At the same time one must realize that probably no act produces only value without disvalue, or conversely. One should do those acts which achieve the values above and avoid those acts which bring about their opposites. One ought to produce freedom instead of servitude, efficiency instead of inefficiency, and happiness instead of unhappiness. Those situations which arise when these values are in conflict present special problems and represent the focal point of this book.

In summary, I assume: (a) that moral philosophy is a meaningful discipline and that moral problems are genuine problems; (b) that something of significance can be said about distributive justice although answers to some of the higher-order questions of value theory are absent; (c) that happiness, liberty, equality, merit, efficiency, and ability are values, i.e., that they are elements of the good life and constituents of distributive justice; (d) that one ought to produce value and prevent disvalue to the extent that it is in one's power.

General outline of the book. The purpose of this book is to work towards a new theory of distributive justice. In the next three chapters, traditional formulas of distributive justice will be developed and criticized. These include utilitarianism, egalitarianism, and socialism. In each case a clear and pre-analytically plausible statement of the principle will be provided. Each of the formulas will then be subjected to philosophical criticism. The purpose of this criticism is not purely destructive, however. The critical analysis of these formulas should accomplish the following purposes:

1. It should make explicit the value conflicts which characterize disputes about distributive justice.

2. It should assist us in isolating the basic values which underlie all dis-
    cussions of distributive justice.
3. It should convince us that no one formula or value can be used by
    itself to provide an adequate account of distributive justice.

In the final chapter, the positive aspect of the book becomes apparent as I try
to synthesize the conflicting values of Chapters II through IV into a coherent
account of distributive justice. To aid me in this task I have adopted as a
heuristic device the Language Model. After a formal principle of distributive
justice is provided, I use this model to provide six substantive principles
to apply in various situations. The overall theory is then elaborated and defended. Moreover, I show how this approach to distributive justice can be
elaborated and specified further. Hence, the discussion makes a start towards
a new theory of distributive justice.

II. Utilitarian Theories of Distributive Justice

THE NONPHILOSOPHICAL discussions of distributive justice which are carried on in parliaments, newspaper editorials, and barrooms reflect an implicit utilitarianism. In an attempt to win their case, the disputants appeal to the public good, the public interest, or the general welfare. Public planners argue that the general welfare resulting from highways, airports, and urban renewal justifies the uprooting of the inhabitants of these sites and the compensated destruction of their property. The welfare of education allegedly justifies the property tax, and appeal to the public interest supports the legislative control of the sale of alcoholic beverages. Utilitarian appeals are a commonplace in contemporary discussions of distributive justice.

The purpose of this chapter is to formulate and examine two utilitarian theories of distributive justice. The first is based on classical utilitarianism and will be referred to as philosophical utilitarianism. The second is based on economic utility and welfare theory and will be referred to as economic utilitarianism. The dialectic of the discussion moves from the inadequacy of philosophical utilitarianism to the general success of economic utilitarianism in meeting the objections to philosophical utilitarianism, and finally to the difficulties of economic utilitarianism when the objections are reformulated. We conclude that utilitarianism properly considers several values which are relevant to the solution to problems of distributive justice, but unfortunately, it ignores or minimizes others.

1. Philosophical Utilitarianism

Philosophical utilitarianism explained. The philosophical utilitarian theory of distributive justice is as follows:

PU: In a set of possible distributions, that distribution which will provide the greatest happiness for the greatest number is the one which is just.

Although an explicit statement of the utilitarian theory of distributive justice is absent in the classical writers,[1] the formulation above is certainly consistent with the view taken by those writers. However, I shall take "happiness" in a somewhat broader sense than Bentham, letting it refer to satisfaction rather than simply to pleasure or the absence of pain. It seems more correct to say that one has maximized satisfaction in winning the race than it is to say that one has maximized pleasure in winning the race. In any attempt to ascertain a just distribution, one must consider the resulting happiness or satisfaction.

In the phrase "greatest happiness," "greatest" is as important as "happiness." Not only are we concerned with happiness but with the greatest balance of happiness over unhappiness. The utilitarian formula is committed to the principle of maxima (efficiency in economic utilitarianism). Both happiness and maximization are factors which should be taken into account in any just distribution. In the language of this book, I shall speak of happiness and maximization as values which one tries to achieve in any just distribution.

The most imprecise phrase in the utilitarian formula is "the greatest number." The purpose of this phrase is to provide considerations of extent of the distribution of happiness into the utilitarian formula. I shall limit considerations of extent to the happiness of human beings. The basic difficulty with the phrase is to determine which human beings are to count and how much they are to count. When one speaks of counting each person as one and only one, the utilitarian formula seems decidedly egalitarian. Equality would become a third value along with happiness and maximization which one tries to achieve in any just distribution. However, the value of equality is not easily accommodated into utilitarian theory. Bentham and Mill both assert and deny its importance in the utilitarian formula.[2] The problem of equality will occupy

1. There are several reasons for this noticeable absence of concern for problems of distributive justice in the classical writers. First, classical utilitarianism developed as a general theory of legislation and morals. Problems of justice were subordinate problems. Secondly, when specific problems of justice were discussed, the interest centered on corrective rather than distributive justice. Bentham's *Principles of Morals and Legislation* is devoted almost entirely to corrective justice. Thirdly, "justice" was often considered synonymous with "equity." Since equity created difficulties for utilitarianism at the outset, it became incongruous to speak of a utilitarian theory of justice. Justice was a problem for utilitarianism, not something to be explained on utilitarian grounds.
2. Both realized that equality may contribute to the greatest happiness; however, it seems that neither considered the value of equality independently of the greatest happiness principle. Bentham speaks of equality as follows: "Equality is not itself, as security, subsistence, and abundance are, an immediate instrument of felicity. It operates only through the medium of these three, especially through abundance and security. Of all three taken together, the use, fruit, and object is felicity—the maximum of felicity; of this maximum the magnitude depends upon the degree of equality that has placed in the proportions in which these three are distributed." This quotation is from *The Constitutional Code* in *The*

our attention later in this chapter and again in Chapter III. For our present purposes, I shall use the phrase "the greatest number" to refer to all human beings relevant to the distribution under consideration, insisting that such human beings should count for something, but leaving it an open question as to how much they should count.

As in classical utilitarianism in general, the utilitarian formula for distributive justice is committed to the view that happiness is measurable. The utilitarian takes the position best exemplified by Sidgwick.

> And of course, here as before, the assumption is involved that all pleasures included in our calculation are capable of being compared quantitatively with one another and with all pains; that every such feeling has a certain intensive quantity, positive or negative (or perhaps zero), in respect of its desirableness, and that this quantity may be to some extent known so that each may be at least roughly weighed in ideal scales against any other.[3]

In order to maximize satisfactions, one must be able to measure and compare them.

Finally, the philosophical utilitarian uses essentially the same method for determining the maximum amount of happiness as the classical utilitarians. One first determines the numerical balance of pleasure over pain for each individual and then one adds the numerical values for each individual together. That distribution which has the highest numerical value of satisfaction is the distribution which is most just. Consider the three possible distributions below:[4]

	I	II	III
Recipient A	10	10	10
Recipient B	−10	− 5	5
Recipient C	5	5	− 2
	5	10	13

Works of Jeremy Bentham, ed. John Bowring (New York: Russell and Russell, Inc., 1962), vol. 9, p. 14. See also *Works* II, 271–2; *Works* III, 228–30, 294.

Two quotations from Mill illustrate this tension even more dramatically: "It (equality) is involved in the very meaning of utility, or the greatest happiness principle. That principle is a mere form of words without rational significance unless one "person's happiness, supposed equal in degree (with the proper allowance made for kind), is counted for exactly as much as another's." . . . All persons are deemed to have a right to equality of treatment, except when some recognized social expediency requires the reverse." John Stuart Mill, *Utilitarianism* (New York: Bobbs-Merrill Company, Inc., 1957), pp. 76–8.

3. Henry Sidgwick, *Methods of Ethics,* 7th ed. (Great Britain: University of Chicago Press, 1962), p. 413.

4. In all such examples, the numerals refer to units of happiness or unhappiness.

According to the utilitarian formula, distribution III is clearly the most just. It contains the greatest amount of happiness for the greatest number, assuming that the happiness of all those relevant has been considered.

Objections. The adequacy of philosophical utilitarianism depends on its ability to surmount internal and external criticisms which can be brought against it. Internal criticisms are questions about the conceptual clarity of the formula, its ability to function as a practical principle of distributive justice, and its consistency. External criticisms are usually presented in the form of counter-examples. Distributional situations are created which if analyzed on utilitarian grounds would be just, but which on the basis of our basic intuitions about justice are clearly unjust. I shall follow this pattern here; however, I shall use as the basis of my counterexamples competing nonutilitarian values. In providing this analysis I am not providing some new and devastating blow to the utilitarian formula. In fact this approach has been strongly influenced by Nicholas Rescher's penetrating criticism of utilitarianism. My strategy, then, is to show that there are other values which conflict with the maximization of happiness, that these conflicting values ought to be taken into account when settling questions of distributive justice, and that these values cannot be accommodated into the utilitarian formula. The underlying criticism is that utilitarianism makes the value of happiness and the principle of maxima the final arbiter of distributive justice at the expense of other values. Hence, the counterexamples I shall use will be of the following form:

1. The utilitarian formula declares as just that distribution which provides for the greatest happiness of the greatest number.
2. However, in distributional situation A, if we distribute according to the greatest happiness of the greatest number, then value x (e.g., individual liberty) will be sacrificed for happiness.
3. If value x is sacrificed for the greatest happiness, then the resulting distribution will offend our most basic intuitions of justice.
4. Therefore the utilitarian formula is incorrect.

My purpose in raising these internal and external criticisms is not to examine in detail the criticisms and utilitarian replies found in the philosophical literature, nor is it to discuss the similarities and differences between classical utilitarians. By presenting the external criticisms from the somewhat novel perspective of competing values, I hope to show why the philosophical utilitarian theory of distributive justice is inadequate. If the objections appear as decisive to others as they do to me, perhaps the utilitarian can be convinced to change his strategy. He should give up philosophical utilitarianism and accept economic utilitarianism as the more adequate utilitarian theory of distributive justice.

Internal criticisms. There are three general types of internal criticism which can be leveled against philosophical utilitarianism. First, the formula itself suffers from a lack of conceptual clarity. Secondly, there is no acceptable method which practically enables us to maximize satisfaction. Thirdly, the formula can, on occasion, be inconsistent. One distribution is just on the principle of the greatest happiness, while another would be just on the happiness of the greatest number.

First criticism—vagueness. Although it seems correct to interpret "happiness" as meaning satisfaction rather than balance of pleasure over pain, the concept of happiness is still conceptually vague. If the utilitarian principle of maxima is to work, then happiness should be a precise quantitative concept. It seems obvious that it is not such a concept. The view that pleasures or satisfactions can be quantitatively determined and compared has been criticized almost to the point of ridicule.[5] How does one determine quantitatively the satisfaction he gets from listening to Beethoven's Fifth Symphony? How does one compare the satisfaction he gets from listening to Beethoven's Fifth Symphony with the satisfaction he gets from contemplating Picasso's *Three Musicians*? When different kinds of pleasure are considered the problem is even more acute. It seems absurd to attempt to make a quantitative comparison between the satisfaction of winning a point in a philosophical discussion and the satisfaction of taking a cool swim on a hot summer day.

Recently some utilitarians have argued that such exact quantification is not required.[6] It is not necessary to assign units of utility to philosophical discussions or to swims. If we know that one is more pleasurable than another, preference ratings are attainable. These preference ratings provide an ordinal, rather than a cardinal, measurement of utility. Allegedly ordinal measurement is sufficient.

Unfortunately, this reply will not do. Consider the following preference ratings for three recipients, R, S, and T for two alternatives *a* and *b*: R prefers *a* to *b*. S prefers *b* to *a*. T prefers *a* to *b*. If the alternatives are exclusive, then the modern utilitarian would argue that *a* should be selected because it produces the greatest happiness for the greatest number. Such a procedure does not guarantee a utilitarian result, however. If R and T only slightly prefer *a* to *b* and S greatly prefers *b* to *a*, the greatest happiness will result if *b* is chosen. Simple ordinal preferences will not supply the detailed analysis required for utilitarian policy decisions.

5. See esp. Wesley C. Mitchell, "Bentham's Felicific Calculus" in *The Backward Art of Spending Money and Other Essays* (New York: Augustus M. Kelley, Inc., 1950), pp. 177–202.

6. Jan Narveson, *Morality and Utility* (Baltimore: Johns Hopkins University Press, 1967), p. 42.

Other conceptual difficulties attend the phrase "the greatest number." It is difficult to decide how many people are relevantly affected by the distribution under consideration. Consider a plant manager who faces the decision of paying his workers a fair wage. Should he limit his consideration only to the type and quality of the work that the men do, or should the family circumstances of the men be considered in his calculation? In addition, there are the effects his wage policy will have in the community; the higher the wage, the greater the happiness of the merchants in the community. However, there is also an effect on the industry as a whole. Could the rest of the industry match his pay increases? Finally, there is the effect of his policy on the national economy and on international trade. Is this proposed pay hike inflationary? Does it upset the country's balance of payments? Clearly the plant manager cannot calculate all these factors exactly when he decides to increase wages. In considering the greatest good for the greatest number, where do his responsibilities end? By what criteria can we judge in any given situation whose happiness should be considered? It is one thing for the philosophical utilitarian to assert that happiness be maximized for the greatest number. It is quite another thing to specify relevantly the phrase "greatest number." If we take the phrase in the strict sense and include everyone, even posterity, the utilitarian formula becomes unworkable. Hence we need a criterion of relevance to decide whose happiness should be considered. It will not help to argue that we should make our decision about whom to include and whom not to include on the basis of the greatest happiness of the greatest number. After all, this is the principle which creates the difficulty. The criterion of relevance cannot be a utilitarian one. The utilitarian is embarrassed on two counts. First, he must supplement his theory by a nonutilitarian criterion of relevance. Secondly, the utilitarian has no such criterion to offer. It is not clear to whom the phrase "greatest happiness" refers.

Second criticism—practicality. The principle of maxima cannot be applied in practical situations. Even if satisfaction could be measured by Bentham's calculus or in some other way, the measurements could never be made because utilitarianism is an open-ended system. It is open ended because there are an infinite number of factors to be considered.

Bentham himself realized the magnitude of the problem. He recognized that one could not assume that all men derived the same satisfaction from a liter of wine. Bentham listed thirty-two separate circumstances, biases of the sensibility, which affect comparisons. In addition, these biases of the sensibility can differ by degree. In fact,

. . . some circumstances are susceptible of perhaps an infinite variety of degrees. . . . of the circumstances of all kinds which actually do attach upon an event it is only a very small number that can be discovered by the utmost exertion of the human faculties; it is a still smaller number that ever actually do attract our notice. . . .[7]

Although Bentham believes he has the necessary tools for measurement, he admits that there are an infinite variety of circumstances affecting satisfaction, and that these circumstances make precise measurement impossible.

G. E. Moore was similarly troubled when he realized the infinite multitude of circumstances which have to be taken into account before one can determine the greatest happiness.

In order to show that any action is a duty, it is necessary to know both what are the other conditions which will, conjointly with it, determine its effects; to know exactly what will be the effects of these conditions; and to know all the events which will be in any way affected by our action throughout an infinite future. We must have all this causal knowledge. . . . we must also possess all this knowledge with regard to the effects of every possible alternative. . . .[8]

Once it is realized that a distribution of happiness is not an isolated act, but that it has an infinite number of effects on the happiness of others both now and in the future, Moore's perplexity can be paraphrased so that it applies specifically to the philosophical utilitarian theory of distributive justice. Clearly we must have some criterion for limiting what is to be taken into account if the utilitarian theory is to be practical.

Moore suggests that utilitarian ethics should limit itself to what is *likely* to produce the greatest total value. This suggestion may be correct, but Moore provides no principle for limiting the effects or consequences that should be considered. Allowances for ignorance do have to be made; certain effects do have to be ignored; however, classical utilitarianism has provided no acceptable indication of how this is to be done.

Recently a step in that direction was made by David Braybrooke and Charles Lindblom.[9] The strategy is known as disjointed incrementalism. The basic principles of the strategy can be rephrased so as to apply specifically to problems of distributive justice. They include the following:

1.   Consider only those distributions whose known or expected consequences differ from each other only incrementally.

7. Jeremy Bentham, *Principles of Morals and Legislation* in *The Utilitarians,* 1832 ed. (Garden City, N.Y.: Doubleday & Company, Inc., 1961), pp. 68, 81.

8. G. E. Moore, *Principia Ethica,* 5th ed. (Cambridge: Cambridge University Press, 1956), p. 149.

9. David Braybrooke and Charles E. Lindblom, *A Strategy of Decision,* 2nd ed. (New York: Free Press, 1967). See esp. chaps. 9 and 10.

2. Consider only those distributions whose known or expected consequences differ incrementally from the *status quo.*
3. Evaluation of the different possible distributions is determined on the marginal or incremental differences of social states rather than through an attempt at a more comprehensive analysis of social states.

However, the strategy is inadequate on two counts. First, an incremental change is never clearly defined; it is not certain what constitutes an incremental change. Secondly, there is no good reason to believe that the just distribution lies in the range of distributions which differ only marginally from the *status quo.* Certainly the long range and potentially larger differences do count on occasion. The strategy of disjointed incrementalism reflects an unjustified concession to conservatism.

Nicholas Rescher adopts a procedure which bypasses these methodological problems of precision and relevance. He attempts to make the problems of distributive justice retrospective rather than prospective.

We are to make essentially retrospective judgments of preference among *wholly defined alternatives* involving human actions together with their *specific* determinate set of (presumptive) consequences, rather than looking upon the evaluation as a historical transaction that itself lies within the course of human events oriented toward a developing open future.[10]

By having wholly defined alternatives, the problem of practicality can be resolved. Although Rescher can adopt this procedure in order to simplify matters for highlighting other objections to utilitarianism, this procedure obviously cannot be used to avoid philosophical problems. To rescue utilitarianism in this way would be to make it irrelevant.

The principle of maxima can be practically applied only if we determine whose satisfaction is to count, what idiosyncrasies might affect the measurement, and how these idiosyncrasies are to be overcome. It is just these practical problems which utilitarianism seems unable to resolve.

Third criticism—inconsistency. The utilitarian formula is internally inconsistent. The two main considerations in the formula, the greatest good and the greatest number, do not always work harmoniously, but can come into conflict. Suppose there are two distributions which would allot happiness as follows:[11]

---

10. Nicholas Rescher, *Distributive Justice* (New York: Bobbs-Merrill Company, Inc., 1966), p. 21.

11. This argument is taken from Nicholas Rescher, *op. cit.*, pp. 25–34. The form of argument for the remainder of this discussion of philosophical utilitarianism is adapted from Rescher.

	I	II
Recipient A	3	2
Recipient B	3	2
Recipient C	3	6
	9	10

The second distribution would provide the greatest total happiness. The first would give greater happiness to a greater number of individuals. Considerations of greatest (total) happiness may often conflict with the extent of the distribution of happiness. As long as both considerations are considered fundamental to the utilitarian formula, there is no way that utilitarianism can arbitrate the conflicts which arise.

These three types of criticism make philosophical utilitarianism vulnerable. First, the formula suffers from conceptual ambiguity. Secondly, the principle of maxima cannot be applied in practical situations. Thirdly, the formula is inconsistent whenever considerations of maxima conflict with considerations of extent.

External criticisms. A common "textbook" criticism of utilitarianism is that it sanctions the sacrifice of an individual for the happiness of the majority. The strength of the objection depends on its ability to establish that the gain in happiness is unjustly obtained at the expense of some other value, e.g., individual freedom. In each of the following counterexamples, I hope to show that the distribution which provides for the greatest happiness of the greatest number is clearly not the most just. Each counterexample will exhibit some other value which should have priority over utilitarian values in this situation. The values are chosen from the list provided in Chapter I.

Consider the following possible distributions:

	I	II
Recipient A	90	62
Recipient B	90	62
Recipient C	90	62
Recipient D	20	62
Recipient E	21	62
	311	310

In the alternatives above, only equality and maximized happiness are relevant. All other complicating factors are ruled out by hypothesis. Although distribution I provides for the greatest happiness of the greatest number, it seems evident that distribution I is not the more just. Equality of distribution is a value and in this case it seems to override considerations of the greatest happiness. Although equality does not always override happiness, in this case our intuition leads us to think that it does. Distribution II is the more just.

If the extra unit of happiness in the counterexample above should cause any difficulty, consider the following distributions where total happiness is equal:

	I	II
Recipient A	12	9
Recipient B	11	9
Recipient C	4	9
	27	27

If we exclude any complicating factors, distribution II is clearly the just distribution. Equality of distribution is a value to be considered, and in this particular case provides the principle for distribution. However, the utilitarian formula, which limits considerations of justice to the greatest happiness of the greatest number, has no means for establishing the justice of distribution II. The objection which this counterexample raises is apparently recognized by the great classical utilitarian Sidgwick.

It is evident that there may be different ways of distributing the same quantums of happiness among the same number of persons; in order that the Utilitarian criterion of right conduct may be as complete as possible, we ought to know which of these ways is to be preferred. . . . In all such cases therefore, it becomes practically important to ask whether any mode of distributing a given quantum of happiness is better than any other. Now the *Utilitarian formula seems to supply no answer to this question: at least we have to supplement the principle* of seeking the greatest happiness on the whole by some principle of *Just* or *Right Distribution* of this happiness. The principle which most Utilitarians have either tacitly or expressly adopted is *equality.* . . .[12]

This quotation is significant because Sidgwick admits that utilitarianism has no basis for selecting distribution II over distribution I, and he also admits that the principle of equality which does provide the basis of selection is supplementary to utilitarianism. This is precisely the point which the counterexample is designed to establish. Other principles are necessary over and above the utilitarian principle to satisfactorily resolve all problems of distributive justice.

My criticism goes far beyond Sidgwick's, however. Utilitarianism may be inadequate even if the quanta of happiness are not the same. Sometimes it is

12. Sidgwick, *op. cit.,* pp. 416-7. Emphasis mine.

more just to provide an equal distribution than it is to provide a distribution for the greatest happiness of the greatest number. This is the point which the first counterexample was designed to establish.

The only way the utilitarian can escape this difficulty is to deny that the value of equal distribution is supplementary to utilitarianism. He would have to argue that equality is built into the utilitarian formula itself. This strategy fails, however. Historically, none of the utilitarians did build egalitarianism into their definitions of utilitarianism. In fact, discussions of equality always enter several chapters after the original definition has been proposed. At one point Mill did assert that equality was part of the *meaning* of utility. However, Mill did not argue for this assertion, and there is not the slightest reason to think that Mill's assertion is correct. Another possibility is to appeal to the phrase "the greatest number." However, there is no necessary connection between distributing according to the happiness of the greatest number and distributing equally. Hence the counterexamples still stand. Utilitarianism neither provides a mode of distributing a given quantum of happiness nor does it allow for the possibility that an equal distribution may be more just than a distribution which provides for the greatest happiness of the greatest number. The utilitarian faces a dilemma. If he disregards equality, philosophical utilitarianism is inadequate as a theory of distributive justice. If he tries to include it, he no longer holds a strict utilitarian position. The correct conclusion to be drawn from this discussion is that both maximum happiness and equality of distribution must be taken into account. What is required is a principle which will enable us to decide when equality is more important than maximum happiness. Obviously, utilitarianism cannot provide that principle.

Other values. A second value which may be considered is the moral character of the recipients. Certain personal characteristics are felt to be relevant in at least some distributive situations. Consider two men, Frank and Joe: Frank is both a loving and a just husband and father; Joe, on the other hand, is just but not loving. Consider the following two distributions:

	I	II
Frank	4	3
Joe	$\frac{3}{7}$	$\frac{4}{7}$

Assume that the two alternatives above are exclusive and exhaustive. Moreover, assume that there will be no future consequences as a result of the distributions; a distribution in favor of Joe will not tend to lessen the quality of love in other husbands and fathers. On these assumptions I is the just distribution. The utilitarian would have no basis, however, for choosing I over II.

Providing Frank and Joe with some additional personal characteristics enables us to expand the point above. Suppose that we endow Frank with a large number of virtuous characteristics and that we endow Joe with a large number of vices. The reader is free to use his imagination here. In light of our additional knowledge of the personalities of Frank and Joe consider the following distributions:

	I	II
Frank	100	100
Joe	101	99
	201	199

On the utilitarian theory, I is the more just because it provides for the greatest happiness of the greatest number. In fact, however, distribution II seems more just. In this case the characteristics of the recipients seem more important than the total happiness. In this case justice is done by rewarding virtuous characteristics rather than by achieving the greatest happiness.

Again the appropriate conclusion to be drawn is that both the greatest happiness and the moral worth of the recipients are values to be considered. An arbitrating principle is needed to settle the conflicts which arise between them.

The value of individual liberty will provide still another example of the strategy. Suppose that we could solve the problem of distribution in a manner which would produce the greatest happiness for everyone while necessitating a drastic limitation of individual free choice. Assume that the loss of freedom does not create unhappiness. Such situations have been described with some literary skill in Huxley's *Brave New World* and Orwell's *1984*. For a society of ten people, the situation can be represented schematically as follows:

	I	II
Happiness:	100 units each	90 units each
Individual Choice:	30% restricted	No change from present
	1,000	900

The utilitarian is committed to distribution I because it provides the greatest happiness for the greatest number. However, distribution II is the just distribution. It would be unjust in this case to increase happiness by curtailing individual freedom. We have another counterexample to the utilitarian principle, another value to be considered, and additional situations in which an arbitrating principle is required.

In summary, internal problems are not the only difficulties which beset philosophical utilitarianism. It falls victim to serious external flaws as well. Numerous counterexamples can be created if we take certain nonutilitarian values and bring them into conflict with the greatest happiness principle in certain distributive situations. In particular, I have provided instances where equality, moral worth, and individual liberty override greatest happiness. In so doing, I have shown philosophical utilitarianism to be too exclusive to be an adequate theory of distributive justice.

If this assault on philosophical utilitarianism has not sunk the ship of greatest happiness, it has left it in imminent danger of sinking. However, some urgent SOS's to its sister ship economic utilitarianism may yet provide some means of rescue. Let us turn to economic utilitarianism in order to determine if it can avoid the fatal difficulties discussed here.

---

2. Economic Utilitarianism

When we analyze the flaws which prove fatal to philosophical utilitarianism, a paradoxical discovery can be made. Philosophical utilitarianism is both too broad and not broad enough. It is too broad because its appeal to the greatest happiness makes it become hopelessly indefinite. It is not broad enough because the problem of distribution is discussed without taking sufficient account of other values. Economic utilitarianism is designed to overcome these difficulties. Moreover, economic utilitarianism has the additional advantage of making reference to the production of goods and services.

Economic utilitarianism—amplified and explained. In this section I hope to indicate the nature of economic utilitarianism. In later sections I will show how the theory mitigates or avoids the criticisms of philosophical utilitarianism, but also how these criticisms can be reformulated so as to raise serious objections to economic utilitarianism as a theory of distributive justice.

Stated briefly, economic utilitarianism asserts that: The principle which should be used for the production and distribution of economic goods and services is to maximize the greatest amount of economic welfare for the greatest number.

There is a definite affinity between this principle of distributive justice and economic utility or welfare theory. One of the founders of welfare economics asserted that:

Pleasure and pain are undoubtedly the ultimate objects of the Calculus of Economics. To satisfy our want to the utmost with the least effort—to procure the greatest amount of what is desirable at the expense of the least that is undesirable—in other words to *maximize pleasure* is the problem of Economics.[13]

Much later I. M. D. Little concurred in this mode of expression. He linked welfare economics and ethical utilitarianism.

If one maximizes those satisfactions which are the effects of economic causes, then one is maximizing, literally, a part of happiness. So long as the process does not involve making any other part of happiness smaller, then it follows that in striving to maximize economic welfare one is doing one's duty.[14]

The purpose of this discussion must be made clear at the outset. I am borrowing from welfare economics to construct a more adequate theory of utilitarianism. I do not contend that an economist need consider this problem; if he should consider it I do not contend that he need consider it in this way.

Economic utilitarianism limits considerations of the maximization of happiness to economic welfare. Economic welfare is generally understood to refer to the happiness obtained from goods and services which can be exchanged for money. Like philosophical utilitarianism, economic utilitarianism has two principles—a principle for maximizing economic welfare, and a principle of extent. Unlike philosophical utilitarianism, these principles apparently can be precisely defined. Optimum conditions of efficiency are necessary for producing the maximum amount of economic welfare. A principle of equality supplements the optimum conditions of efficiency. Using maximization of happiness and equality of distribution as values, the two following rules for increasing economic welfare can be adopted.

R_1: If the size of the national income is increased, provided that distribution is not altered, then the economic welfare of the community will be increased.

R_2: If the distribution of the national income is made more equal without diminishing the total amount of that income now or in the future, the welfare of the community will be increased.[15]

13. Stanley Jevons, *Theory of Political Economy,* 4th ed. (London: Macmillan and Co., 1911), p. 37.
14. I. M. D. Little, *A Critique of Welfare Economics,* 2nd ed. (Oxford: Clarendon Press, 1957), p. 8.
15. These rules are slightly modified versions of those put forth by Cecil Arthur Pigou in *Wealth and Welfare* (London: Macmillan and Co., Ltd., 1912), pp. 20-4 and in *The Economics of Welfare,* 3rd ed. (London: Macmillan and Co., Ltd., 1929), pp. 72, 78.

Hence economic welfare is maximized when goods are most efficiently produced, when they are equally distributed, and when efficiency does not inhibit equal distribution or conversely.

With respect to maximization, we can more precisely formulate the conditions of efficiency than we could with Bentham's formula. A few definitions and axioms enable us to state the optimum conditions for efficiency given the natural resources and state of technology at the time.

Definitions:

D_1: Total utility = df   the satisfaction provided by the consumption of any economic good or service or collection of goods and services.

D_2: Marginal utility = df   the extra unit of utility added by one extra unit of an economic good.

D_3: Marginal product = df the extra output or product added by one extra unit of a factor, while other factors are held constant.

D_4: Marginal cost = df   the extra cost incurred when you produce one extra unit of output in the cheapest way possible.

Axioms:

A_1: An individual tries to maximize his utility.

A_2: As the amount of a good consumed increases, the marginal utility of that good tends to decrease. (Law of diminishing marginal utility)

A_3: As one factor of production is added, while all other factors are held constant, total production will increase but by diminishing amounts. (Law of diminishing marginal products)

Optimum Conditions of Production and Consumption:

C_1: Consumer satisfaction is maximized when the marginal utility of all goods with respect to their prices is equal.

$$\frac{MU_1}{P_1} = \frac{MU_2}{P_2} = \cdots \cdot \frac{MU_n}{P_n}$$

C_2: Production is achieved at least cost when the marginal physical products per last dollar spent is equal for all the factors of production.

$$\frac{MPP_1}{P_1} = \frac{MPP_2}{P_2} = \cdots \cdot \frac{MPP_n}{P_n}$$

C_3: Output is maximized when output is increased up to that point where marginal cost equals price.

Maximum output occurs when MC = P

We shall refer to the conditions above as the optimum conditions for economic efficiency.[16] Optimum conditions have a central position in all welfare economics from its founding to the present. An informal explanation of C_1, C_2, and C_3 should provide an intuitive justification of them.

C_1 simply asserts that people should spend their income so that they are equally satisfied with everything they buy. People should not spend so much for an automobile that they find themselves unable to buy the clothing, education, and travel they desire. The automobile would become too expensive relative to clothing, education, and travel. Happiness would be maximized if a little less were spent for the automobile and consequently more could be spent on the others, i.e., if the marginal utilities of all goods with respect to their prices were equal.

C_2 states formally the common-sense principle that a businessman will use that combination of factors which will produce the most at least cost. Suppose that the rent of a machine equals that of a laborer; they are both $3 an hour. If the marginal physical product of the machine is greater than that of the laborer, the entrepreneur will substitute machines for men up to that point where the marginal products are equal. He will see that he gets the same marginal product with respect to prices for all factors of production.

C_3 provides the optimum condition for plant output. Suppose that the appliance industry is perfectly competitive, that the price of an alarm clock is $10 and that the cost of producing another alarm clock is $8. Clearly the industry would produce another alarm clock and keep producing alarm clocks until the point where the production of another equals the price of the clock, i.e., until marginal cost equals price.

We now turn to the principle of equality which is the basis of R_2. A discussion of equality brings us to a more controversial area. Discussions of equality

---

16. Recently economists have replaced the marginal utility analysis of optimum conditions by revealed preference analysis. I retain the older analysis because of its relevance to the problem of distributive justice. Each of the conditions can be derived mathematically. For a formal presentation of optimum conditions the reader is directed to Milton Friedman, *Price Theory, A Provisional Text* (Chicago: Aldine Publishing Company, 1962) and George Stigler, *Theory of Competitive Price* (New York: Macmillan Company, 1942). For the relation of optimum conditions analysis to welfare economics, the reader is directed to Abba Lerner, *The Economics of Control* (New York: Macmillan Company, 1944); M. W. Reder, *Studies in the Theory of Welfare Economics* (New York: Columbia University Press, 1942), and Paul Samuelson, *Foundations of Economic Analysis* (Cambridge, Mass.: Harvard University Press, 1947).

of distribution are not usually part of the mainstream of economics. Recently even welfare economics has minimized the problem of distribution and emphasized production exclusively. However, at this point we shall discuss the traditional position of Marshall and Pigou. There are three distinct advantages in doing this:

1. We start at the beginning, by considering welfare economics in its traditional form.
2. By considering distribution, we do not make the mistake of ignoring distribution as philosophical utilitarianism ignored production.
3. The principle of equality gives a precise formulation of the extent of distribution which was not explicit in philosophical utilitarianism.

The argument for the equality of distribution is as follows:

1. Assume that everyone has the same capacity for satisfaction and is faced with the same set of prices.
2. With constant prices, as total income increases, after some point the marginal utility of income decreases. (A_2 applied to income). In other words, an extra dollar will yield less satisfaction to a man with more money than it will to one with less money.
3. Therefore an equal distribution of money income will yield the greatest sum total of satisfaction.[17]

Accepting the analysis of economic utilitarianism above, one can conclude that economic welfare is maximized for the greatest number when the optimum conditions of production and consumption prevail, when the distribution of income is equal, and when there is no conflict between the optimum conditions of production and the equal distribution of income.

I shall now test this theory against the objections which proved fatal to philosophical utilitarianism.

The traditional objections and economic utilitarianism. Economic utilitarianism has two advantages which should enable it to overcome the objections against philosophical utilitarianism. First, the economic utilitarian formula for maximization is very precise. The utility calculus for optimum conditions has, in the hands of economists and mathematicians, become highly formalized. It was just this lack of formal precision which created the difficulties for philosophical utilitarianism.

Also, economic utilitarianism considers the dynamic factor of production. The means to economic happiness are not waiting to be plucked—they must be produced, and it is production which economic utilitarianism emphasizes.

17. For the present we shall ignore economic difficulties with this argument.

By emphasizing an ever-expanding quantity of goods and services, economic utilitarianism seeks to bury the touchy issues of distribution raised against philosophical utilitarianism in an avalanche of economic goods.

Internal objections. With respect to the first internal objection, economic utilitarianism seems clearer and more precise. This results from limiting the concept of happiness to economic happiness and by defining economic happiness as that satisfaction which can be obtained from those goods and services which can be purchased for money. This is the approach taken by welfare economists.

> Hence the range of our enquiry becomes restricted to that part of social welfare that can be brought directly or indirectly into relation with money.[18]
> In this book, the economic causes of change in the happiness of an individual are taken to be those things and services which the individual consumes or enjoys, and which could be exchanged for money, together with the amount and kind of work which an individual does.[19]

This approach, if certain assumptions are made, enables money to serve as an approximate measuring rod for happiness.[20] For example, if Jones and Smith have the same income, and Jones spends $100 on x and Smith spends $100 on y, then we can presume that Smith and Jones are equally happy. Similarly, if z is offered at an auction at which Jones will bid only $100 for z while Smith will bid $200, we can say that z will make Smith twice as happy as Jones. Although certain technical problems exist with this conception, it does reflect our ordinary ways of speaking. We often say that Jones gets as much happiness from spending his recreation money on the movies as Smith does spending his on the concerts. In economic utilitarianism, happiness is so defined that quantitative measurement becomes possible.

Some might object that this precision is only gained by changing the nature of the problem. Utilitarianism is concerned with happiness as a whole, while economic utilitarianism is concerned only with economic happiness. This objection is not very serious, however. Most of the elements of happiness which are not given a money value cannot be distributed in any case. Love is an element of general happiness but not of economic happiness. It cannot be bought and sold. However, it is of such a nature that it makes no sense to speak of distributing love. If an economic utilitarian cannot distribute it, a philosophical utilitarian cannot distribute it either. If most of the elements

---

18. Pigou, *Economics of Welfare*, p. 11.
19. Little, *op. cit.*, p. 6.
20. This is the position taken by Marshall. See Alfred Marshall, *Principles of Economics*, 8th ed. (New York: Macmillan Company, 1952), p. 131.

omitted by economic utilitarianism are like love, philosophical and economic utilitarianism do converge in problems of distributive justice.

If Pigou's analysis is followed, the phrase "the greatest number" is also precisely defined. Distribution should be made so that the money income is equal for the people involved. We now know how much each person is to count if happiness is to be maximized.

Secondly, much of the force of the second internal objection is overcome. Although some problems may remain, the fact that optimum conditions analysis is amenable to highly sophisticated mathematical techniques limits this type of objection to a great extent. The definitions, axioms, and theorems of optimum conditions analysis provide a more precise method than Bentham's calculus for achieving the greatest happiness. Moreover, new advances in mathematics and computer programming theoretically enable economists to gauge the effects of changes in one aspect of the economy on other aspects. For example, they could gauge the effect of a 10 percent increase in the production of steel on other dependent products and on prices. This mitigates the difficulty of measuring vast effects of an act. Furthermore, by considering workers as a factor of production, a relation between production and distribution is established. We can measure the contribution the worker makes to production and compensate him accordingly. This means of compensation provides a built-in method for determining which individuals are relevant with respect to some proposed distribution. Economic utilitarianism has the theoretical framework to decide questions of relevance and hence can mitigate the objection which proved so effective against philosophical utilitarianism.

Equality and welfare. The internal objection which Pigou's economic utilitarianism cannot avoid is the conflict between maximization and extent. Recall that Pigou has two rules for an increase in economic welfare (p. 25), which may be paraphrased as:

R_1: Welfare is increased if the total amount of goods and services is increased without affecting distribution.

R_2: Welfare is increased if equality of distribution is increased without decreasing the total amount of goods and services.

However, increases in the total amount of welfare are related to the optimum conditions. In order to achieve maximum efficiency with respect to a given job, each worker should be paid according to his efficiency. Only if all workers are equally efficient on that job, should compensation be equal. However, people are not equally efficient. For this reason conflicts can occur.

If one insists on equality, then a smaller amount of goods and services will be produced. If one insists that the total goods not be reduced, then some inequality is necessary.

Most economists have accepted this conflict, but Pigou has argued that ultimately there is no conflict. Before abandoning Pigou's theory, some attention should be given to his argument:

1. Any transference from rich to poor, regardless of the effect on total dividend, will benefit the poor for that year.
2. (1) however, does not imply that such benefits remain over the long run.
3. Savings depend solely on national dividend plus accumulated stores from previous years.
4. Other things being equal, therefore, any dimunition in the amount of the dividend in one year lessens the supply of capital with which labor can cooperate in the following year.
5. In that year, therefore, both the national dividend and the real earnings of labor are reduced below what they otherwise would have been.
6. If the transference continues, the process of reduction initiated in this way is continuous and cumulative. In the next year real earnings are reduced still further below that level and so on.
7. Therefore, the advantage of the increased real income of the poor, which an act of transference brings about immediately, can only prove an advantage on the whole, if the act does not involve an injury to the magnitude of the national dividend.[21]

Economists would challenge the argument on economic grounds; however, I shall assume that the economics is correct. I wish to explore the implications of the argument. Pigou's analysis shows that equality violates the optimum conditions. Pigou should have concluded his argument as follows:

7'. Therefore, the advantage of the real income to the poor, which an act of transference brings about immediately, will upset the optimum conditions of production and ultimately will work to the disadvantage of the poor.

However, this conclusion makes R_2 superfluous. It is superfluous because Pigou's argument shows that in practice a more equal distribution would upset the optimum conditions and in the long run make an increase in welfare impossible. R_2 would only apply in the unlikely case where all workers

21. Pigou, *Wealth and Welfare*, p. 294.

on a given job are equally efficient. In this case, however, equality is deducible from the statement of optimum conditions and R_2 is not required. R_2 would be significant only if welfare could be increased by more equality of distribution even if total national income decreases. Pigou's argument is an attempt to show that such a situation does not occur. Either we must leave equality out of consideration or we must admit that the demand for equality will often conflict with the demand for the maximization of total income. Most economists have omitted considerations of equality and have allowed distribution to be dependent on the optimum conditions. The motivating factors for this move are not our concern here. However, if we should follow this move, the conflict between efficiency and extent will be avoided. The third and final internal objection would be surmounted. To follow the economists at this point, however, would create an obvious difficulty. To omit considerations of equality and make distribution dependent on the functioning of the optimum conditions of analysis would seem to make economic utilitarianism even more vulnerable to the counterexamples dealing with equality in Section 1. Let us turn to these external criticisms and see if economic utilitarianism could plausibly eliminate the value of equality altogether.

External criticisms. The strategy of this approach is to allow distribution to resolve itself automatically as a result of the operation of the optimum conditions and the laws of supply and demand. The distribution of income is determined by competition for the factors of production and by the efficiency of each factor. The competition itself results from the attempts of industry to satisfy the demands of the consumer.

It must be emphasized that this approach is not the same as that of the "New Welfare Economics" which began with Pareto and continued in various forms through much of the 1940's. This can be easily seen if we examine briefly three variations of the New Welfare approach, the Pareto criterion, the Kaldor-Hicks compensation criterion, and the Social Welfare Function.[22]

Pareto Criterion: A situation X is better in terms of economic welfare than a situation Y, when at least one person is better off at X than at Y and no one is worse off.

Kaldor-Hicks Compensation Criterion: A situation X is better in terms of

22. These three principles can be found in the following articles: Vilfredo Pareto, *Manuel D'economie politique,* trans. Alfred Bonnet (Paris: V. Girad & E. Briere, 1909); J. R. Hicks, "The Foundations of Welfare Economics," *Economic Journal* XLIX (1939) 696–712; Nicholas Kaldor, "Welfare Propositions in Economics," *Economic Journal* XLIX (1939) 549–552, and Abram Bergson, "A Reformulation of Certain Aspects of Welfare Economics," *Quarterly Journal of Economics* LII (1938), 310–334.

economic welfare than a situation Y if at least one person is better off at X than at Y and if no one is worse off or if any loser could be (or actually is) compensated out of the gains of the winners.

Social Welfare Function: A situation X is better in terms of economic welfare if a *given* social welfare function is more efficiently achieved in situation X than in situation Y.

The inadequacy of the views above is seen when we reconsider the counterexamples from Section 1.

	I	II	III	IV
Recipient A	90	62	12	9
Recipient B	90	62	11	9
Recipient C	90	62	4	9
Recipient D	20	62		
Recipient E	21	62		
	311	310	27	27

If the Pareto criterion were adopted, economic utilitarianism would be too limited to be an adequate theory of distributive justice. On the Pareto criterion there are no cases in which one could say that welfare had increased if someone was worse off than before. It certainly could not be used to justify a move from I to II. The Pareto criterion implicitly accepts the current distribution of income and is limited to expanding economies.

The compensation criterion tries to avoid the restrictiveness of the Pareto criterion. According to the Kaldor-Hicks criterion we could move in the first pair above from II to I since the gainers could compensate the losers and one extra unit of happiness would still remain. However, in the second pair, if we start from IV and move to III, we could compensate but then we would be back to IV. But suppose we start at III and move to IV. Again we could compensate, although we would end up at III again. The point is that we ought to move from III to IV but not from IV to III, other things being equal. The Kaldor-Hicks criterion either has nothing to say here or it would justify either move. However, the situation is more serious still. Suppose the proposal was to move from I to II. According to the Kaldor-Hicks criterion the move ought not to be made because the gainers D and E could not compensate the losers, A, B, and C. Clearly, however, the move from I to II ought to be made, other things being equal. The Kaldor-Hicks criterion is prejudiced in favor of the *status quo*. In point of fact, the present distribution serves as a norm. But why should the gainers compensate the losers, if the gainers are the poor and the losers are the rich? What difference does it make that the gainers could compensate the losers if the losers are the poor and the gainers are the rich? If we begin with a situation of great inequality, the Kaldor-Hicks criterion falls victim to the same type of counterexample raised against philosophical utilitarianism.

The social welfare function approach is designed to avoid these difficulties. The social welfare function is to be given from outside, by ministers or philosophers or more likely by politicians. According to this criterion we should move from II to I if (a) I more efficiently maximizes the welfare function, and (b) if equality is not an element of consideration in that given function. This way of looking at the problem greatly helps economists since it enables them to do their theoretical work without a great concern for the ethical assumptions. Obviously, this approach cannot provide a moral theory of distributive justice.

Another approach. Another approach an economic utilitarian might take justifies the lack of concern with equality by arguing that the alleged counter-examples are misconceived. One should only move from I to II if everything else is equal. Similarly one should only adopt distribution IV over distribution III if everything else is equal; however if the production of the goods and services is considered, everything else cannot be equal. Once the factor of production enters the picture, the counterexamples lose their force. First, the economic utilitarian can show that in many cases inequality can be justified. Secondly, even in some cases where it is not completely justified, equality is really not important anyway.

In the discussions which are to follow, the dialectic ends with the advantage in favor of the economic utilitarian. This advantage ends when the more sophisticated objections are developed later in this chapter.

There are good reasons why distributions I and III may be more just than II and IV. Inequality is necessary if the optimum conditions of production are to be fulfilled. The inequality of money income is necessary to provide the incentive for the work required to produce the large quantity of goods and services required. It is often argued that a society cannot adopt the principle of equal distribution because no one would have an incentive to work harder than anyone else. Inequality is necessary as an incentive for production. Moreover, those workers who have skills which are in short supply and large demand will receive more income. Hence strict equality would upset supply and demand and result in a frustration of consumer happiness.

Finally, if the optimum conditions are violated year after year to provide for equality, output will be reduced and there will be less for everyone. The results of continual distribution by equality can be hypothetically illustrated by the table below.

	Year 1	Year 2	Year 3	Year 4
Recipient A	4	3	2	1
Recipient B	4	3	2	1
Recipient C	4	3	2	1
Recipient D	4	3	2	1
Recipient E	4	3	2	1
	20	15	10	5

If this diminishing supply of the goods for economic happiness could be avoided by inequality, clearly it would be just to do so. Equality of distribution is simply a slogan if there is very little to distribute. It is considerations such as these which enable Lord Robbins to argue "there is nothing ethically compelling in a total divorce between earnings and pecuniary value of contribution to the social product."[23]

Even if one admits that the arguments above present strong justification for inequality, one might argue against the economic utilitarian that his argument is not conclusive. First, wages are tied too closely to consumer demand. What a man earns depends in large part on what makes others happy. When consumer demand enables a rock 'n' roll performer to earn ten times the income of a fine classical musician, it is not obvious that this distribution is just. Secondly, people capitalize on unique skills to obtain exorbitant incomes. Such cases of economic rent where an athlete or actor can demand fantastic salaries for a skill which is to a large extent a biological accident are not clearly just. Thirdly, some people take advantage of accidents of nature. A natural disaster can make some people rich. A blind guess in the stock market may yield a fortune. However, the resulting distributions may more appropriately be called unjust than just. The common occurrence of situations like these limit the appeal of economic arguments for inequality.

The economic utilitarian has a ready reply to this objection. If he were a philosopher he might structure his argument as follows:

1. I admit that there are certain situations which offend one's concern for the value of equality and which cannot be justified by arguments for inequality in that situation.
2. But, some offensive situations are inevitable in an economic system where supply and demand play a large part.
3. However, the results of the system as a whole are so beneficial that everyone is better off. For example, a system which produces the

23. Lionel Robbins, "Equality as a Social Objective" in Politics and Economics (London: Macmillan and Co., Ltd., 1963), p. 79.

means for twenty-four units of happiness and distributes them unequally, twelve, seven, and five, is more just than a system which
produces only six units of happiness and distributes them equally,
two to each.

4. (3) is true even if we feel that the recipient of five units should
have received more in that particular system.

5. Hence problems of distributive justice must be seen in the total context.

6. Therefore, a given instance of an unjust distribution is not an effective counterexample against the theory. The system of distribution
may make everyone better off, including the offended party, than any
alternative system.

The idea behind this argument reflects the basic position of United States
economic policy. The problem of inequality is resolved by increased production. While speaking of former President Johnson's Great Society Program,
James Tobin put the matter most succinctly:

> The Great Society is not a redistributive program. President Johnson does
> not raise the question of distributive justice as between rich and poor,
> capital and labor. He does not propose a different Deal of the same cards,
> whether Square, or New, or Fair. He proposes to solve the pressing prob-
> lems of society—poverty, education, health, etc.,—out of the vast annual
> increments of the national product and without enlarging the govern-
> ment's share of the national product. The emphasis is on an ever-grow-
> ing pie, rather than a slicing up of a given pie in a new way.[24]

The guiding idea behind both theory and practice is that a few unjust instances of distribution can be overlooked if the economic system provides an
ever-increasing abundance of the means to economic happiness, surpasses alternative systems, and makes those who are unjustly treated in some particular
instance better off in the long run.

Some of this analysis has been accepted in a recent paper of John Rawls.[25]
He thinks that it is a mistake to try to establish justice for individual distributions. Instead a social contract should be provided which provides just
institutions. An institution is just if it makes the least-favored as well off
as they can be. Any distribution which results in a society of just institutions
is *ipso facto* just. "This account of distributive shares is simply an elaboration

---

24, James Tobin, *National Economic Policy* (New Haven: Yale University Press, 1966),
p. 42.
25. John Rawls, "Distributive Justice" in *Philosophy, Politics, and Society,* ed. Peter Laslett
and W. G. Runciman, 3rd series (New York: Barnes & Noble, Inc., 1967), pp. 58–82.

of the familiar idea that economic rewards will be just once a perfectly competitive price system is organized as a fair game."[26]

An economic utilitarian would be sympathetic to Rawls's approach because the inequality of a given situation is more than justified by the great increase in productive capacity and the resulting benefits to all. Hence the economic utilitarian can reply that although his theory is not perfectly equitable in every situation, the theory still provides a principle for just distribution. This reply can be rephrased in the language of this book as follows: Even if the economic utilitarian emphasizes the value of efficiency at the expense of the value of equality, he might still have a just theory of distribution. The counter-examples to this position are inadequate because they fail to take into account (a) that inequality is a necessary condition for the most efficient production of the means of happiness, and (b) the resulting increased productivity more than offsets inequality, and provides more benefits even to the offended parties than any alternative system.

Other values. If the above arguments are accepted, economic utilitarianism has hurdled the formidable equality objection to philosophical utilitarianism. For complete success, however, economic utilitarianism must consider the other values listed in Chapter I which *prima facie* should be considered in any just distribution. The economic utilitarian must show that his theory accommodates these values, as happiness and efficiency are accommodated, or he must show that these other values can be overlooked, as he did with the value of equality.

Certainly the economic utilitarian recognizes the value of skill or ability. Those with the highest skills in any endeavor produce the greatest marginal product in that endeavor and hence they receive a higher income. One's own happiness depends on his ability to use his skills to satisfy the happiness of others.

Moreover, the economic utilitarian would argue that he recognizes the value of individual choice. He would challenge the notion that his theory would either justify or make possible a 1984. A man makes his own decision as to what goods and services will make him happy. He uses his income to bid on the open market so that the goods and services he desires are in fact produced. The economic productive system structures itself around those goods and services which provide individual happiness. The economic term, consumer sovereignty, refers to this consumer freedom. The consumer decides what will make him happy and hence what the economic system will produce.

Finally, the economic utilitarian has a reply to the counterexample based on the moral worth of the recipient. The economic utilitarian can insist that

26. *Ibid.,* p. 78.

the emphasis on production does enable him to consider the moral worth of the recipient in any actual distribution. John deserves more income than Sam if (a) John works more than Sam, (b) John works more efficiently than Sam, or (c) John has an ability or skill which is more in demand than Sam's. Depending on the circumstances, (a), (b), (c), or some combination thereof will justify distributing more income to John than to Sam. In each case above John is rewarded because he makes a larger contribution to the welfare of others than Sam. Certainly if one makes a greater contribution to the welfare of others, it is reasonable to conclude that he ought to receive more. Moreover, merit, in the sense outlined above, is rewarded naturally by the efficient economic system. This is one of the happy cases where efficiency and merit coincide.

However, suppose a critic of economic utilitarianism uses "undeserving" to refer to popularly undesirable activities which the recipients might engage in, such as producing tobacco or alcohol or winning bets at the horse races. The economic utilitarian must admit that such activities might be highly rewarded on economic grounds even though some people would argue that the reward is most unjust. A liquor store owner could be a most successful businessman if economic utilitarianism prevailed. However, such success would provide a reason for the Christian Temperance Union to consider economic utilitarianism unjust. Disputes such as these raise some of the most difficult problems in a philosophical discussion of distributive justice. Since the distribution of income depends to a large extent on what other people want produced, it is always open for a critic of economic utilitarianism to say that certain desires ought not to be fulfilled or that the order of individual desires should be changed. Hence public service workers do not consider their lower salaries just simply because their services are not in high demand. People ought to pay teachers, firemen, and social workers more, not less, than actors, popular singers, and prostitutes. The critic would argue that an economic system which bases income distribution on production and production on consumer desire is certain to be unjust. People do not always choose wisely; their sense of values may be "mixed up." This type of objection is not without merit and it rightly causes the economic utilitarian some discomfort.

However, the economic utilitarian does have a reply to this criticism. If the individual consumer's preference is not to be the criterion for what is produced, whose preference is to decide what is really good and ought to be produced? Should the government, or psychologists, or philosophers make that decision? Not only does the critic have difficulty in finding some objective means for judging what ought and ought not to be produced, but if such an objective judging system could be found, it could only be instituted at the expense of some people's freedom of consumer choice. Those who find popular entertainment of singers more desirable than the services of social workers will lose their power of consumer sovereignty. The economic utilitarian may reasonably argue that the dangers of tampering with individual choice far outweigh the danger that some group may suffer from the unreflective and unsophisticated desires of others. Unless someone can produce a generally accepted standard of what ought to be produced and in what order of priority, the critic's objection is not decisive. The economic utilitarian accepts people's desires at face value; he measures merit the only way he can—in terms of productive efficiency and consumer demand for skills and services. One may feel uncomfortable with this, but one would feel even more uncomfortable if a group of philosophers, politicians, or psychologists decided and enforced their view about what ought to be produced and according to what priorities.

Prima facie economic utilitarianism is more adequate than philosophical utilitarianism as a theory of distributive justice. It not only surmounts the internal criticisms, but it is sufficiently complicated to take account of all the relevant values which should be achieved in distributive justice and hence it can surmount the external objections as well. In this system:

1. The goal is to maximize the greatest amount of economic happiness by producing the most at least cost.
2. The consumer freely decides which goods will give him happiness.
3. Optimum conditions provide the required efficiency. Under these conditions skill or ability is rewarded.
4. A recipient is considered morally worthy if he works hard, efficiently, and possesses a skill which aids in the satisfaction of consumer desire.
5. (1) through (4) can only be achieved at the loss of some equality in distribution, however, this loss of equality is more than justified. It is a small price to pay for the great benefits which result.
6. Should one argue that certain intrinsically bad economic activities are rewarded, the economic utilitarian need only reply that there are no standards for determining what is intrinsically bad.

In this way, economic utilitarianism considers all of the values which are considered important as factors of a just distribution. By emphasizing production, the counterexamples against philosophical utilitarianism are shown to be misconceived and hence are readily surmounted. If economic utilitarianism is inadequate, more sophisticated variations of the traditional objections are required.

Sophisticated objections. The strategy here is the same as that used against philosophical utilitarianism—internal objections will be considered first, then external objections. A word of caution is necessary at this point. Some of the material to follow, especially the discussion of utility theory and the theory of optimum conditions, raises complex and sophisticated questions of economics. Even though my discussion is limited to those aspects of the problem which are relevant to economic utilitarianism as a moral theory of distributive justice, in some cases I must accept well-informed economic judgment without raising all the complexities or settling the issues once and for all. The interested reader is referred to the various notes for references to some of the purely economic and/or more complex issues involved.

Internal objections. One of the alleged advantages of economic utilitarianism was the ability to use money as a measuring rod for comparing satisfactions. Hence, if Smith and Jones each spent $100 for item *x*, it was assumed that Mr. Jones and Mr. Smith derived equal satisfaction from item *x*. This assumption was challenged by the economist Lionel Robbins on the basis that the conclusion that Jones' satisfaction equaled Smith's was a statement of value and not a statement of fact.[27] To draw this conclusion one must make the value judgment that Smith and Jones have equal capacities for satisfaction. Robbins's analysis was so influential that many economists did give up the view that satisfactions could be interpersonally compared. Robbins's question as to the place of value judgments in economics lies beyond the scope of this book. It is obvious, however, that the introduction of value judgments creates no special difficulties to this discussion. The problem to be faced here is the plausibility of:

1. Jones's satisfaction from bread is measured by the amount he paid for it.
2. If Jones and Smith both willingly pay 25¢ for bread, they derive the same satisfaction from bread.
3. You can add Jones's satisfaction from bread to Smith's satisfaction in order to determine the total satisfaction for bread.

With respect to (1), Jones's satisfaction for bread is not accurately reflected by the price he pays for it. Under optimum conditions, the price of a good depends on the value of the last unit. However, according to the law of diminishing marginal utility, the earlier units provide more satisfaction than the later units. Since price is figured on the basis of the last unit, the consumer enjoys a surplus.[28] Consumer's surplus can be most readily illustrated by a bulk item like sugar or salt. Suppose we buy a five-pound bag of sugar. If the cost of the last pound is 12¢, the sugar will sell for 60¢. However, if only one pound of sugar were available, the buyer would be willing to pay more than 12¢ for it.

27. Lionel Robbins, *An Essay on the Nature and Significance of Economic Science,* 2nd ed. (London: Macmillan and Co., Ltd., 1935), pp. 136–8.
28. Paul Samuelson, *Economics,* 5th ed. (New York: McGraw-Hill, Inc., 1961), p. 446.

The purchase in five-pound lots provides a consumer surplus. To get an accurate measurement of the actual satisfaction, one would have to figure the marginal utility of each unit separately. Hence (1) must be appropriately qualified.

The plausibility of (2) requires that Smith and Jones have comparable tastes. Suppose that Smith really enjoys a certain kind of bread, but that Jones buys it simply to please his wife. Can we reasonably assume that Smith's satisfaction from the bread equals Jones' satisfaction from pleasing his wife? If this situation causes the reader no special difficulty, consider the situation where bread forms a staple of Jones's diet, but that Smith is sufficiently wealthy that bread is simply marginal to the roast beef and wine which he enjoys. Certainly Jones's and Smith's satisfaction are not equal. Statement (2) holds only if Jones and Smith have approximately the same taste and income.

The most serious difficulties, however, are reserved for (3). One of the fundamental criticisms of economic utility theory is that it is wrong to speak of total utility as the sum of individual utility. There is no summation process for adding satisfaction. There is no method which enables us to discover total welfare or the greatest economic happiness. Suppose, for example, that a change in the price level should occur so that candy becomes expensive and cereal relatively less expensive. This means that the satisfaction of those who consume candy will decrease, and the total satisfaction of those who consume cereal will increase. Clearly the loss of satisfaction of the candy consumers must be deducted from the gain of satisfaction to the cereal consumers if we are to learn whether total satisfaction has increased or decreased. Here it seems money is the only appropriate measuring rod, but unfortunately that measuring rod may prove inadequate. If the cereal buyers are poor and the candy buyers rich, money cannot be used accurately as a measuring rod in this case. The slight increase in extra money for the poor as a result of the lower cereal price will be more noticeable and provide a greater amount of happiness, than the slight loss in money for the rich. If the change in price means that the rich have 6¢ less and the poor 6¢ more, one cannot say that there has been no total change in satisfaction. The satisfaction of the poor outweighs the loss of the rich, even though the monetary changes are equal. Money, as a measuring rod, changes its shape when applied to different groups. You cannot add the satisfactions of the rich to the satisfactions of the poor to arrive at total satisfaction. These problems have been summarized in an informal way by I. M. D. Little.

> The statement "I am about to add together the difference which this change would make to Smith and Jones and compare the result with the difference it would make to Brown," sounds like nonsense. It sounds like nonsense because addition is a precise mathematical operation which re-

quires the possibility of counting. There is no way we can measure units of satisfaction, and so count them.[29]

If we assume that the criticisms raised by economists have some merit, then an interesting philosophical point results. The same type of criticism is raised against economic utilitarianism as was raised against philosophical utilitarianism. The concept of happiness is too vague and imprecise to admit of the precise quantification which the theory demands. Just as the vagueness of happiness created difficulties for Bentham's calculus, the vagueness of economic happiness creates difficulties for the mathematical application of utility theory.

Two escapes. Before we leave this objection, one should briefly consider two related attempts to avoid the problem above. The first attempt was to abandon the cardinal measurement of utility for ordinal measurement. Under this procedure we no longer say that a commodity gives Smith ten units of happiness and Jones twenty units. We say only that the commodity makes Jones happier than Smith. This change of procedure has no affect on the analysis of the economic problem of equilibrium. The same results can be dervied from either cardinal or ordinal theory. With respect to the utilitarian conclusions of welfare theory, however, the ordinal procedure seems too restricted. Although it can tell us that Jones is made happier by *a* than by *b* and by *b* than *c*, it gives no information on the extent of preference. This is illustrated below:[30]

MOST PREFERRED		LEAST PREFERRED
1. ____ a ____ b ____ c ____		
2. ____ abc _____		
3. ____ a ____ bc _____		
4. ____ a ____ b ____ c _____		

Ordinal theory is unable to conclude which of the above four possibilities best represents S's preferences. From this, we can easily construct the objection utilized against the modern philosophical utilitarian. If two men of three prefer one alternative to another, we cannot conclude that a decision in favor of the majority will maximize happiness. The intensity of the preferences must be considered, and it is the intensity which the ordinal measuring procedure seems to ignore.

29. Little, *op. cit.*, p. 53.
30. This example is adopted from Nicholas Rescher, "Notes on Preference, Utility, and Cost," *Synthese* XVI (1966), 332–43.

Economists have criticized the ordinal procedure as well. Some proofs have been attempted which try to show that ordinal analysis is not sufficient for the derivation of welfare conclusions.[31] The essence of the proof is to show that they are sufficient for deriving conditions of equilibrium, but that they are not sufficient for deriving conditions for maximizing happiness. More recently, much discussion has arisen about considerations of risk in welfare decisions.[32] If this feature is added, it is generally admitted that cardinal, not ordinal, analysis is required. Whatever the advantages of ordinal analysis to positive economic science, the moral philosopher is led to conclude that ordinal analysis is not adequate for his purposes. We still face the problem of a theory which demands quantification but which has no concept of happiness amenable to such precise quantification.

A more radical attempt to avoid the problem of measurement is to give up the concept of maximizing happiness. Instead of referring to maximizing happiness, one speaks of the revealed preferences of consumer choice. Instead of saying that S is more satisfied by x than by y, one says that S prefers x to y. However, the notion of maximizing utility comes to have a radically different meaning.

> Thus the interpretation of the postulate that utility is maximized is simply that the man must behave in the way in which he said he would behave. Roughly speaking maximizing utility means telling the truth—or, less paradoxically, being able correctly to predict one's own behavior.[33]

It is obvious that we no longer have a theory of economic utilitarianism as defined in this chapter. The value of happiness disappears. In philosophical terms, we would move from the problems of measuring happiness to the metaphysical problems of choice. The appropriate conclusion to this discussion is that economic happiness and philosophical happiness suffer from similar vagueness. The concept is not amenable to the precise quantification required by the theory.

Practicality. The second objection to philosophical utilitarianism was that the principle of maxima could not be practicably applied. Too many complicating situations had to be taken into account. The precision of the optimum conditions analysis is alleged to avoid this difficulty. However, I hope to show that

31. Oscar Lange, "The Determinateness of the Utility Function," *Review of Economic Studies* I (1934), 224.
32. See W. E. Armstrong, "Uncertainty and the Utility Function," *Economic Journal* XLVIII (1948) 1–10, and Milton Friedman and L. J. Savage, "The Utility Analysis of Choices Involving Risk," *Journal of Political Economy* LVI (1948), 279–304.
33. Little, *op. cit.,* p. 25.

this precision is obtained only at the cost of realism. So many unrealistic assumptions are required by optimum conditions analysis that economic utilitarianism cannot serve as a theory of distributive justice.

With the aid of four definitions and three axioms, three conditions for the attainment of efficiency were provided. What assumptions must be granted so that these conditions may apply to the real world? The first condition stated that consumers maximize happiness when the marginal utilities of all goods they purchase with respect to prices are equal. This condition assumes the existence of economic men, perfectly rational, completely knowledgeable of all alternatives, and capable of making their selection in the marketplace independently. Of course, there is not the slightest reason to believe that actual consumers behave in this way. They often do not even know what will provide them with genuine satisfaction, and they certainly fail to maximize their happiness. In addition, the pattern of consumption of one person has important effects on others (external economies or diseconomies of consumption). If my consumption of x causes displeasure to others, the optimum conditions are violated. Happiness is not maximized even if the marginal utilities are equal. For example, the playing of radios in crowded places has serious diseconomies. In order to resolve the conflict, at least someone's ability to maximize his satisfaction will be less than optimum.

> The presence of such external effects upsets the optimum conditions of exchange, and it ceases to follow that a fixed stock of goods is ideally distributed if sold at a single price which equates supply with demand. . . .[34]

Finally, there are many goods and services to which the marginal analysis does not apply. It does not apply to a certain class of goods and services in the private sector called indivisibilities, and it does not generally apply in the public sector. The difficulty in the private sector arises with those expensive durable good items like automobiles, appliances, and furniture which are seldom bought. Little puts the problem clearly:

> Thus we cannot plausibly say that an individual brings the rate at which he is willing to exchange a car for a radiogram into line with their relative prices. If consumers really could, and did, do this with respect to all goods, it would follow that it would be impossible ever to raise the price of any superior good without every individual reducing his purchases. This is manifestly not the case.[35]

Little's point is that the consumer cannot reduce his consumption of these expensive infrequently purchased items by a marginal amount when faced

34. *Ibid.*, p. 133.
35. *Ibid.*, p. 167.

with a small increase in price. One does not buy color televisions the way he buys sugar.

Public goods like fire and police protection, defense, and parks create special problems. These goods have the characteristic of nonappropriability. Nonappropriability may be defined as that property of some good which makes it impossible by ordinary market conditions to charge the full cost and to assess the true desire for it. Many public goods have this characteristic because they must be consumed equally by all; those who do not pay cannot be excluded from the benefit. Police protection is available to all whether they pay for it or not. Hence any "rational" individual will understate the full satisfaction he receives from police protection in order to contribute less to the costs. As Paul Samuelson and others have pointed out, this adversely affects the optimum condition that requires equality between marginal rates of substitution and marginal rates of transformation. To charge individuals a uniform price equal to marginal cost is not efficient in the case of public goods.[36] When people attempt to maximize their satisfaction without paying the costs, the optimum conditions break down.

Similar difficulties arise when we consider production. Both the laborer and the entrepreneur are assumed to be economic men. Laborers must be sufficiently rational to move from an area where wages are low to an area where wages are high. As a matter of fact, people are reluctant to leave family and friends in order to receive a slightly higher wage. In addition, we must assume that there are no external economies if the optimum conditions of production are to hold. In actuality, external diseconomies are a commonplace. The public is just now fully appreciating the existence of such diseconomies as air and water pollution, offensive odors and noise. Of course, the economic utilitarian would argue that an ideal pricing system would take all this into account, but no ideal pricing system exists, and the considerations raised above show how difficult it is to devise one. One always tries to overstate losses and understate the benefits so that his particular contribution can be reduced.

The doubts raised about the realism of C_1 and C_2 already undermine the realism of C_3 because of the relation between them.[37] For this reason C_3 is subject to all the unrealistic assumptions raised above. In addition there is a new problem with respect to the policy of marginal cost output. This policy

36. Paul Samuelson, "The Pure Theory of Public Expenditure," *Review of Economics and Statistics* XXXVI (1954), 387–9; "Diagrammatic Exposition of a Theory of Public Expenditure," *Review of Economics and Statistics* XXXVII (1955), 350–6; and "Aspects of Public Expenditure Theories," *Review of Economics and Statistics* XL (1958), 332–8; and William J. Baumol, *Welfare Economics and the Theory of the State,* 2nd ed. (Cambridge, Mass.: Harvard University Press, 1965).
37. A discussion of the relation of these three conditions in the language of marginal substitutability is found in Little, *op. cit.,* chap. IX, pp. 152–65.

rests on the condition that human factors should be paid, if there is no marginal taxation, the values of their marginal products. Since the proportional income and general sales tax are marginal taxes, they would have to be abandoned since they would disturb the leisure-commodity optima by reducing the net real wage below the marginal product of labor.[38]

For optimum conditions C_1 through C_3 to hold, at least the following assumptions must be made:

1. All individuals are economic men, free from ignorance, satisfaction maximizers, and mobile.
2. There are no external diseconomies of production or consumption.
3. Indivisible private goods and most public goods are omitted from discussion.
4. There is no marginal taxation.

Some of the restrictiveness of the assumptions above might be avoided if it could be shown that a situation in which more optimum conditions are satisfied is superior to one in which fewer are satisfied. The aim would be to satisfy as many optimum conditions as possible, an attempt to achieve a second best as it were. This general theory of second best has apparently been successfully challenged in an important article by R. G. Lipsey and K. Lancaster.

> . . . If there is introduced into a general equilibrium system a constraint which prevents the attainment of one of the Paretian conditions, the other Paretian conditions, although still obtainable, are, in general no longer desirable. . . . if one of the Paretian optimum conditions cannot be fulfilled a second best optimum is achieved only by departing from all other conditions . . . Specifically, it is *not* true that a situation in which more, but not all the optimum conditions are fulfilled, is necessarily or even is likely to be superior to a situation in which fewer are fulfilled.[39]

Since the economic issues are so complex, a philosopher cannot conclude with great authority that the objections are decisive. However, it does seem reasonable to conclude that the precision of the optimum conditions has been gained at the expense of realism. The widespread controversy about the adequacy of the fundamental assumptions of welfare economics and the general abandonment of traditional utility theory for revealed preference theory lead the moral philosopher to conclude that there is something to these internal objections. In fact, they seem to count decisively against economic utilitarianism as a theory of distributive justice.

38. The leisure-commodity optima is a special case of C_1. For a discussion see Little, *op. cit.*, pp. 133–4.
39. R. G. Lipsey and Kelvin Lancaster, "The General Theory of the Second Best," *Review of Economic Studies* XXIV (1956–7), 11–32.

External objections. The strength of economic utilitarianism was its ability either to justify the elimination of certain nonutilitarian values or to accommodate them when spelling out the functioning of the market and the conditions for maximum efficiency. This procedure should be examined again.

With respect to equality, the economic utilitarian has two basic arguments: (a) A large degree of inequality is justified. (b) Although the inequality of a given distribution is not justified, it will be justified by the performance of the economic system in the long run. The loss of equality is a small price to pay for the gains in productivity.

Although this defense seems to be a plausible one, there are serious difficulties. To admit that a given situation is unjust is to make an important concession. The only way this particular distribution can be overlooked is to appeal to the long run. The difficulty with this appeal is that it retains some of the static concepts which plagued philosophical utilitarianism. As John Maynard Keynes so cheerfully reminded us, in the long run we are all dead. It may be just to distribute eight units to one man and two units to another in order that tomorrow one can distribute twenty units to the one and fifteen to the other. It may be unjust to distribute eight units to one man and two units to another so that their great-grandchildren may recieve twenty and fifteen units respectively. The philosophical point is a simple one. It is simply not true that all individual unjust distributions can later be rectified by the increasing cornucopia of economic goods. Certain basic economic necessities must be provided now, not later. Secondly, the future can only justify the past if the individuals are the same in both cases.

Further difficulties arise when we recall the unrealistic assumptions required for economic efficiency. If, in the real world, economic production is always considerably below the optimum, the concern for equality takes on new importance. For certain groups in society, the long run becomes very long indeed. The existence of incurable pockets of poverty has received scholarly attention in such works as Harrington's *The Other America.* The existence of incurable poverty has also been documented in a less scholarly, but in a more dramatic way on the streets of our largest cities. Economic utilitarianism must face the fact that there are some problems of poverty which increased productivity alone cannot seem to remedy.

As a matter of practice, welfare economists have made an important concession to the demands of equality utilizing the concept of a welfare floor. One adopts a welfare floor if there is a minimum standard of living below which no member of the society is allowed to fall. Some minimum standard of equality is guaranteed. The addition of the concept of a welfare floor is an important addition to economic utilitarianism. However, the addition is not made on utilitarian grounds. The welfare floor is not adopted because it will provide the greatest economic welfare. Rather, it is a concession to the value of equality in certain distributive situations. Economic utilitarianism cannot be the sole principle of distributive justice because sometimes the value of equality predominates over the value of the greatest happiness.

Other values. As for the values of skill, liberty, and moral worth, the economic utilitarian insists that they be given their due consideration when the conditions for the working of the marketplace are spelled out. Each value occupies a place in that complex system which provides for the greatest happiness. This way of putting the problem betrays the economic utilitarian's weakness. These values are not considered autonomously; they are relevant only when they contribute to the greatest happiness.

A skill is rewarded *only* when it is in demand. If a master of one of the fine arts is not in demand, his share of the economic welfare is diminished. Historians of the fine arts can provide many examples of an artist's standard of living falling below subsistence, hastening his death. Certainly it is not just to make the reward for skills depend only on demand. An artist should receive compensation for his skill whether he is popular or not. Only then is skill given due consideration in discussions of distributive justice.

The economic utilitarian argues that the moral worth of the recipient is given due consideration because his wage depends on (a) the time one works, (b) the efficiency with which one works, and (c) the extent to which his work is in demand and hence on his contribution to the welfare of others.

Unfortunately, the economic world gives too much weight to condition (c) in evaluating moral worth. There are countless numbers of people who work hard and efficiently, although their share of economic welfare is very low. In the moral world, conditions (a) and (b) are more important. If not, moral worth would depend too much on the whim of the desires of others. The economic utilitarian is too quick to identify satisfaction of desire with economic welfare. He is too quick to forget the quality of what is produced. The sale of drugs, firearms, and alcohol is regulated regardless of desire. Once these concessions are made, it is easy to widen the concern for the quality of what is produced when the evaluation is made. A hardworking and efficient bartender may earn more than a hardworking and efficient social worker because the former is more in demand. However, if the quality of the product is considered, it is not at all clear that this is a just distribution. The economic utilitarian's view of moral worth is too limited.

The economic utilitarian tries to meet these difficulties by appealing to consumer freedom of choice. Individual freedom becomes a predominant value. The philosophical theory of freedom which underlies this position and the criticisms of consumer sovereignty are reserved for Chapter III. We must point out at this point, however, that those who have low incomes find their freedom greatly restricted. They do not have the opportunity to select from a wide range of goods and services, but are forced to spend their income on necessities. Often they find it difficult to even provide the necessities. To extol their consumer sovereignty is a mockery. Moreover, individual liberty is not given autonomous consideration in economic utilitarianism. If the optimum conditions are to be obtained, a man's job, the hours he spends on it, and the location of his work depend far more on economic factors beyond his control than on any decision of his own. As Little points out correctly:

> It must decrease the economic welfare of a particular individual if we force him to work where he does not want to, or if we give him an all or nothing choice as to the amount of work he does. The balancing of the claims of free choice for actual workers against the advantages of increased production is a matter towards the decision of which the static theory of welfare seems to give us little help.[40]

At least on the production side, individual liberty is not incorporated into the utilitarian system.

It seems appropriate to conclude that economic utilitarianism still unjustifiably excludes the value of equality and unsuccessfully attempts to accommodate the other values. The more general conclusions which may be drawn from this long and tedious discussion are as follows:

1. Philosophical utilitarianism is inadequate as a theory of distributive justice.
2. The precision of economic utilitarianism and its concern for production is an improvement over philosophical utilitarianism. Perhaps philosophers should attempt to improve economic utilitarianism and abandon some of the outdated issues.
3. However, the utilitarian formula sacrifices realism for precision and fails to give due consideration to competing nonutilitarian values. The utilitarian formula is not sufficient as a formula of distributive justice.
4. However, the utilitarian values of happiness and efficiency must necessarily be considered before any conclusion as to what constitutes just distribution can be made. Any theory which omits them is inadequate.

Because the value of equality has traditionally caused difficulty for utilitarians, let us turn our attention to this value. Perhaps an egalitarian formula can provide an adequate theory of distributive justice.

40. Little, *op. cit.,* p. 154.

III. Egalitarian Theories of Distributive Justice

ONE OF the most influential appeals in disputes concerning distributive justice is the appeal to the value of equality. The emotive force of an appeal to this value has the power to effect revolutions to overthrow the prevailing economic order. Philosophically, however, the concept of equality is one of the vaguest concepts in social philosophy and philosophical discussions of equality are notorious for their ambiguity. Equality functions extremely well as a political slogan; it functions very poorly as a philosophical concept.

In spite of the ambiguity surrounding the concept, the importance of equality in questions of distributive justice has been established in Chapter II. The purpose of this chapter is to formulate concisely and then to evaluate the adequacy of various egalitarian formulas of distributive justice. The early sections in this chapter will be devoted to the egalitarian formulas. The final sections will focus on an overall egalitarian position and on the dispute between egalitarian theories of distributive justice and libertarian theories of distributive justice. Hopefully, the analysis in the first five sections prepares the way for a sharper and more decisive discussion of this conflict than is usual.

The dialectic of the argument proceeds as follows: The discussion begins with two egalitarian principles of distribution. Here the concern is with the equal distribution of commodities. The third egalitarian principle is a formal egalitarian principle. It may refer either to equal distribution or to equal treatment. In this section, there is a transition as I move from equal distribution to equal treatment or equal rights. The last two principles of distributive justice refer to equal rights. The transition from equal distribution of commodities to equal rights plays an important part in the dialectic of the argument. The five egalitarian formulas which constitute the basis of our discussion are the following:

E_1: For any commodity x, the just method of distribution is to divide x equally.

E_2: Although individual commodities may be distributed unequally, the just distribution of income is the equal distribution.

E_3: Whatever criterion is chosen for distribution, with respect to that criterion equals should be treated equally and unequals should be treated unequally.

E_4: There are certain values to which men have an equal right. If some commodity u is a necessary condition for the achievement of some value y, then it should be distributed so that the equal right is achieved.

E_5: Everyone has an equal right to a minimum standard of living. All commodities should be distributed so that this equal right is achieved.[1]

I do not contend that equality has no role to play in distributive justice. Rather I only contend that an egalitarian formula or position is not sufficient for the achievement of distributive justice. That is, an egalitarian position cannot resolve some difficulties which could be considered problems of distributive justice, and it is assumed that some other theory could solve these problems.

1. Equal Distribution

Neither E_1 nor E_2 is a serious candidate for an adequate principle of distributive justice. Under E_1 all commodities would be distributed equally. Obviously, however, most commodities ought not to be distributed equally. Medicine should go to the sick, food to the hungry, gasoline to automobile owners, etc. The distribution of particular commodities must always be made with reference to individual needs, i.e., with reference to well-being or happiness.

By limiting E_2 to total income, the egalitarian frees himself from the necessity of distributing all commodities equally. Under E_2 a person is free to spend his equal share of total income on any commodity or set of commodities he desires.

The proposal that income should be distributed equally is highly inadequate as well, however, since important considerations relevant to just distribution are overlooked. The moral worth of the recipient is not considered. Both the lazy and the industrious would receive the same reward. Moreover, no consideration is made for ability or skill. Excellence of performance would receive

1. This list is highly representative, but not exhaustive.

no special reward. Traditionally, this type of proposal has been attacked because it overlooks the requirements of efficiency. On the traditional economic view, an equal distribution of income would cripple the incentive for efficient production, upset the maximum conditions for production, and produce a dwindling supply of goods and services. Finally, as with E_1, due consideration is not given to happiness or well-being. Suppose that Jones is suffering from an acute illness which requires an expensive operation and a lengthy postoperative recovery. To recover from this illness Jones would not only have to spend his entire share of the total income on this operation but he would have to go into debt as well. Certainly in this case E_2 would not provide a just distribution. Jones's special situation entitles him to a share of the total income which is greater than, not equal to, the others. With respect to well-being, E_2 makes no allowance for ill fortune. Those who fall victim to accident or disease must spend their equal shares of the total income on absolute necessities while their more fortunate fellow human beings spend a far larger portion of their equal shares on luxuries. Certainly this situation does not represent a just distribution. The above considerations demonstrate the inadequacy of E_2 as a principle of distributive justice.

This conclusion produces a paradoxical situation. It is commonplace to criticize existing distributions on grounds of equality. However, egalitarian positions such as E_1 and E_2 which utilize substantive principles of equal distribution are open to readily recognizable objections which are clearly accepted by all. We find ourselves in the embarrassing situation of demanding that income be distributed equally, but that the share of some is to be more equal than the share of others. Perhaps a different kind of egalitarian formula would resolve the paradox.

2. Formal Equality

E_3 *as a principle of equal distribution.* One of the most common means of resolving the paradox is to make the egalitarian formula purely formal. Something like E_3 has recently been defended by Sir Isaiah Berlin.[2] According to E_3, a distribution x is just only if equals are treated equally and unequals, unequally. Unlike E_2, nothing is said about the actual distribution of income. There is no specific reference to actual divisions of income at all. E_3 is a purely formal egalitarian principle. Such a limitation provides a ready response to the

2. Isaiah Berlin, "Equality" *Proceedings of the Aristotelian Society,* LVI (1955–6), 301–26.

objections raised against E_2. In each case, distribution may conform to some value x so long as equal possessors of that value are treated equally. Specifically, E_3 allows us to maintain first, that equal efficiency earn equal reward; secondly, that equal moral worth merits equal reward; thirdly, that equal ability deserves equal income; and fourthly, that equal needs require equal means of satisfaction. Since E_3 is only a formal principle of distributive justice, it is compatible with any substantive principle of distribution. E_3 restricts the distribution only to the following extent: If the distribution is to be made on the basis of x and if S and T possess x equally, then the distribution should be equal.

Objections. Even if E_3 should be acceptable as an egalitarian principle, it cannot provide an adequate theory of distributive justice. Because the principle is merely formal, it cannot be used to make substantive moral decisions about particular distributions. Neither can it arbitrate between conflicting substantive positions. For example, a formal principle cannot arbitrate between need and efficiency. To make these essential decisions, one must go beyond the formal principle. Hence, if egalitarianism is limited to formal principles, it cannot provide an adequate theory of distributive justice.

Furthermore, the genuine egalitarian would insist that the value of equality play a material and substantive role, rather than a merely formal one, in questions of distributive justice. He would insist that equality has a more important role than that of being merely a constraining condition. Just what the nature of this material role should be is a matter for further discussion.

The difficulties which plague the formal egalitarian position are not limited to sins of omission. On E_3, if S and T are equal with respect to the relevant criterion, then they should receive equal shares. However, this position is open to counterexamples. I refer to these counterexamples as "all-or-nothing situations." Suppose that two men are trapped on an ice floe which will provide minimum subsistence for only one man. Suppose also that both men are equal in all relevant respects. In such a situation an equal distribution of goods is unjust even though both men are equal in the relevant respects. To follow the E_3 principle would doom them both.

Furthermore, this type of all-or-nothing situation is more common than the counterexample would lead one to believe. The growing population problem presents an almost indefinite number of counterexamples of the all-or-nothing type. *Prima facie* everyone has a right to utilize the highways, to sunbathe on a public beach, to fish in a public stream. Soon, however, these public facilities will be so crowded that certain citizens will be excluded even though they have an equal claim to the accommodation. Living space can only be subdivided to a certain point. If we take some pessimistic experts seriously, the situation is also critical with respect to food. The population could grow to such an extent that it would be impossible to provide minimum sustenance for all. At this point, the ice-floe situation would apply to humanity as a whole.

The all-or-nothing situation also occurs whenever there is an indivisible commodity for which people have an equal claim. Suppose that two couples have an equal claim to the adoption of a child; they are both equally qualified to be parents. As King Solomon demonstrated in another context, the baby cannot be cut in two and divided between them. Many commodities simply cannot be divided up equally. In such cases, the principle cannot be followed. Even if S and T are equal in the relevant respect, they should not or cannot receive equal shares. If E_3 is meant to be a formal principle for the equal distribution of commodities, it fails.

E_3 *as a formal principle of equal treatment.* Perhaps the counterexamples presented by the all-or-nothing situations can be avoided if we limit our discussion to equal treatment. In this case, we should say that if S and T are equal in some relevant respect M, they deserve equal treatment. The situation may not be such that they can have equal shares, but at least they deserve equal treatment. We can illustrate this interpretation of E_3 by adapting one aspect of John Rawls's very influential account of justice.[3] One of Rawls's principles of justice is that ". . . inequalities are arbitrary unless it is reasonable to expect that they will work out to everyone's advantage, and provided the positions and offices to which they attach, or from which they may be gained, are open to all."[4]

Rawls's principle is tied to the notion of rules. The inequalities are justified if they are in accordance with the rules and if everyone agrees that the rules will work to everyone's advantage. For example, suppose that there were six bottles of beer to be distributed between S and T and that S and T are equal in all relevant respects. Suppose further that both S and T require four bottles to achieve their goal of pleasant intoxication. If we utilize E_3 this goal would be impossible for both S and T. However, suppose they agree to flip a coin, the winner receiving four bottles. In this case the distribution would still be just even though the distribution was unequal. Each party's consent to the rules justifies the unequal distribution. As Rawls says,

> A practice is just or fair, then, when it satisfies the principles which those who participate in it could propose to one another for mutual acceptance under the aforementioned circumstances (not forced to accept rules which he does not regard as legitimate).[5]

3. John Rawls, "Justice as Fairness," *Philosophical Review* LXVII (1958) 164–94. It is stressed that the following discussion is an adaptation of Rawls's position.
4. *Ibid.,* p. 165.
5. *Ibid.,* p. 178.

For Rawls, equal treatment is achieved by equal citizenship and it is the task of each citizen to indicate his support or nonsupport of the rules. "To satisfy the concept of justice, there must exist in society a position of equal citizenship within which the liberty of the person is secured. . . ."[6] On the basis of this concept of equal citizenship, an egalitarian might reformulate E_3 as follows:

E_3': A distribution x is just only if it is according to rules adopted by equal citizens.

Objections. The difficulty with this view is the ambiguity of "equal citizens." Suppose that all citizens are equal in the sense that they have one vote. If a decision is to be made with respect to some rule, each citizen will have one vote expressing either approval or disapproval for the rule. If the majority decides, then rules for distribution could be adopted which are clearly unjust. A majority of equal citizens could enact legislation which would deprive the minority of a just share of the distribution.

Suppose we reject majority decision for just this reason and adopt, as Rawls apparently does, a unanimous voting procedure. In this case, inequalities are justified if they are in accordance with rules which have been accepted by every citizen.

This requirement seems too strong, however. Any one person could refuse to accept a rule simply to obtain special privileges for himself.[7] If one person is capable of frustrating a proposal desired by the majority solely for the purpose of selfish gain, it seems that the citizens do not have equal voting power. The dissenter's vote is more than equal to the others. His one vote effectively nullifies all the others.

Of course, everyone does have the right to exercise his veto power, and in this respect they are equal. However, this type of egalitarian formula is without practical application. A formal egalitarian theory of equal treatment or equal citizenship is useless unless we have a means for establishing the rules. A unanimity rule for equal citizenship is completely impractical. A majority decision on the principle of "one man–one vote" can lead to injustice. Although a formal principle of equal treatment is superior to a formal principle of equal distribution, the former is incomplete. It seems that what is required is a means for spelling out in what sense people are equal citizens or in what

6. John Rawls, "Constitutional Liberty and the Concept of Justice," *Nomos VI Justice,* ed. Carl Friedrich and John W. Chapman (New York: Atherton Press, 1963), p. 112.
7. Rawls attempts to avoid these difficulties by insisting that the contractees will be ignorant of their final position. A thorough discussion of the problem of effective voting procedures can be found in James M. Buchanan and Gordon Tullock, *The Calculus of Consent* (Ann Arbor: University of Michigan Press, 1962), pts. II and III.

sense they deserve equal treatment. In doing this we would surrender the formal principle, however. Such specification would mark a transition from a formal principle of equal treatment to a substantive theory of equal rights. At this point, however, E_3 is inadequate to provide a formula of distributive justice. Interpreted as an equal principle of distribution or as an equal principle of treatment, it is incomplete. Moreover, the former is vulnerable to counter-examples.

3. Transition

The discussion immediately above marks an important transition in my account of egalitarianism. The inadequacy of E_1, E_2, and E_3 raises serious questions about an egalitarianism based on equal distribution. What seems required if egalitarianism is to be plausible is a theory of equal rights which will determine what distributions are just. Such an egalitarianism need make no appeal to equal distribution at all. The purpose of this section is to illustrate how such a theory of equal rights can be relevant to the problem of distributive justice. Many egalitarians faced with the kinds of difficulties raised against equal distribution have in fact made this transition. However, they seldom make their transition clear to the reader. They seem reluctant to surrender the principle of equal distribution. This reluctance leads to confusion when such phrases as "equitable inequality" are used in the discussion. The following passages illustrate this transition and the vagueness which frequently accompanies it.

> So long as I am at a disadvantage as compared with most people, equity demands that I receive special treatment to remedy the disadvantages. But in so doing equity is not overriding equality. The claim of equity in these circumstances is a claim for equality, not for inequality.
> There appears to be inequality only because the means required in these circumstances to give me equal treatment is different from that employed for the other people.[8]
> The basis of the claim of special need is really a recognition of a claim of equality.[9]
> Since needs are often unequal, this looks like a precept of unequal distri-

8. David Daiches Raphael, "Equality and Equity," *Philosophy* XXI (1946), 126.
9. David Daiches Raphael, "Justice and Liberty," *Proceedings of the Aristotelian Society* LI (1950–1), 189.

bution. But this is wrong. It is in fact the most perfect form of equal distribution.[10]

Each of the quotations moves away from equal distribution. It is clearly recognized that in certain cases equal distributions will not provide distributive justice. In fact, such equal distributions would be unjust. However, it is also evident from the quotations above that the authors are reluctant to give up egalitarianism because of the special circumstances. I believe their reluctance is justified; however, I believe their attempt to save the appearances is unjustified. To infer that the unequal distribution to provide for unequal needs is the "most perfect form of equal distribution" is to seriously confuse the issue. The second quotation is a complete mystery until "equality" has been defined. If "equality" refers to equal distribution, it is certainly not clear that unequal treatment is really a recognition of the claim of equality.

An interesting possibility that can be obtained from all the quotations is that the egalitarian theory of equal distribution may have to be given up. It is not the principle of equal distribution which is so important, but rather it is equal claims which affect how distributions are to be made. A more adequate egalitarian formula might be provided if we emphasize equal rights and de-emphasize equal distribution. Once we speak of equal rights, however, other values become relevant. Pure egalitarianism is then given up. Men are not simply equal; they are equal in certain respects. Once we specify the sense in which they are equal, we introduce additional values into the discussion. The difficult task for the egalitarian is to accommodate these nonegalitarian values into an egalitarian formula. An examination of one implicit attempt to achieve this task provides the necessary groundwork for our discussion of the final egalitarian formulas, E_4 and E_5.

Vlastos's theory. Implicitly, Gregory Vlastos provides this attempted accommodation in a recent interesting and provocative article.[11] Although what is to follow may not represent the explicit intent of the article, I believe it is a fair statement of the position of the article. Moreover, this interpretation is extremely useful for our purposes.

Vlastos began with a specific problem for any egalitarian position: How can one admit that special needs require unequal distributions and still maintain an egalitarian position? Vlastos concludes that provision for special needs is not an exception to the principle of equality but rather the perfect form of equal distribution.[12] To defend his position he utilizes the following example:

10. Gregory Vlastos, "Justice and Equality," in *Social Justice,* ed. Richard Brandt (Englewood Cliffs, N.J.: Prentice-Hall, Inc., 1962), p. 40.
11. *Ibid.,* pp. 31–72.
12. *Ibid.,* p. 40.

We are to assume that an inhabitant of New York City gets a note from Murder Inc. threatening his life. The protection of this particular New Yorker requires a large amount of police manpower and equipment. This man needs a greater amount of police protection than any other man in New York City. However, this inequality of protection is perfectly consistent with the principle of equality because all New Yorkers have an equal right to well-being. In this case, provision of the equal right requires an unequal distribution. It is not equal distribution per se, but equal rights which are important. An equal distribution is not necessarily a just distribution. A distribution which provides for equal rights is a just distribution.

Vlastos accepts two equal rights statements—equality premises, as he calls them. Each man has (a) an equal right to well-being and (b) an equal right to freedom. In this way Vlastos is able to tie equality, liberty, and happiness together into two principles and to use these principles to determine specific distributions. Moreover, Vlastos believes that he can derive efficiency and merit from these two equality premises. Vlastos's discussion of efficiency is too complicated to be presented here. However, his derivation of considerations of merit from the equality premises provides a sufficient example of his method. His argument is as follows:

1. All men have an equal right to well-being. (Premise)
2. If men have an equal right to well-being, then they have a right to the greatest amount of well-being possible. (Previously derived conclusion)
3. If reward with respect to merit provides the highest amount of well-being, then merit is a legitimate consideration in distributive justice. (Conclusion)
4. Reward on the basis of merit does provide a stimulus to the highest amount of well-being. (Fact)
5. Therefore merit is a legitimate consideration.
6. All men also have an equal right to freedom. (Premise)
7. To restrict distribution according to merit is to restrict one's freedom to bestow praise. (Fact)
8. Therefore merit is a legitimate consideration.[13]

The intent of Vlastos's argument is clear:

I have taken the maxim "to each according to his merit" as in need of justification and have undertaken to derive it from a set of propositions which includes only egalitarian value premises plus one or more factual premises.[14]

13. *Ibid.,* pp. 65 ff.
14. *Ibid.,* p. 69.

Objections. Vlastos's account is not without its difficulties, however. First, he does not distinguish between pure egalitarian value premises and mixed value premises. Neither premise (1) nor premise (6) are pure egalitarian value premises. Men are equal with respect to well-being and freedom (happiness and liberty). The values of happiness and liberty are as important in these premises as is the value of equality. We could just as well refer to premises (1) and (6) as hedonistic and libertarian premises respectively. It is misleading for Vlastos to refer to them as equality premises and to argue that he has derived the maxim "to each according to his merit" from egalitarian value premises. Vlastos clearly does not have a pure egalitarian theory.

Secondly, Vlastos fails to develop his implicit distinction between equal distributions and distributions based on principles of equal rights. He does not specify how equal rights to well-being and freedom affect the principles of actual distributions. Vlastos is completely confused about the relation between equal distribution and equal rights. The issue is completely distorted when he says,

> Since needs are often unequal, this looks like a precept of unequal distribution. But this is wrong. It is in fact the most perfect form of equal distribution.[15]

In most cases, if equal rights are achieved, the distribution will not be equal. Once the egalitarian position has been shifted to one of equal rights, the egalitarian must show how equal rights determine distribution. For example, suppose that the supply of goods is inadequate to provide for equal rights. How should the scarce commodities be distributed? Many of the significant problems of distributive justice occur at just the point where the supply of commodities is inadequate to meet legitimate claims. An egalitarian must not only be concerned with distribution according to equal rights, but he must also have something to say on the method of distribution to be employed when equal rights cannot be honored.

Thirdly, Vlastos does not provide any principle for arbitrating disputes which might arise in the application of his "equality" premises. If one seeks to obtain equality of well-being, Jones might get more than Smith, but if one seeks to preserve equality of freedom, then Smith might have more than Jones. This conflict between the principles of equality of well-being and equality of freedom is often misleadingly referred to as the dispute between equality and freedom and represents one of the most troublesome problems in social and political philosophy. Vlastos proceeds as if the problem never existed.

However, Vlastos does provide a promising conceptual framework for formulating E_4.

15. *Ibid.,* p. 40.

4. Egalitarianism and Equal Rights

On the basis of our discussion in Sections 1 to 3, I conclude that there is no pure egalitarian formula which is adequate as a principle of distributive justice. Moreover, I conclude that there are two possibilities for egalitarian positions. The traditional position with respect to distribution is equality of distribution. Either income or certain goods are to be distributed equally if justice is to be done. My own thinking is that this emphasis is misplaced. First, the equal distribution principle is highly vulnerable to objections, as the previous discussion has indicated. Secondly, in most cases, equal distribution per se has no moral advantage over any other method of distribution. Often the dispute about equal distribution is simply a "red herring." What is really at issue is equal rights. To what do men have an equal right? I conclude that the principle of equal distribution should not serve as the basic egalitarian principle of distributive justice. If goods or income should be distributed equally, this can be derived from some other distributive principle. When no such derivation is forthcoming, I conclude that goods need not be distributed equally.

The alternative. An alternative egalitarian position is a political one of equal rights. This position insists that everyone has a right to certain values, and at the distributive level distributions should be ordered so that these equal rights can be achieved. This position finds expression in such statements as "All men have an equal right to life, liberty, and the pursuit of happiness." If one adopts this position as the relevant egalitarian position for distributive justice, the principle of equal distribution properly recedes into the background. Equality of rights does not entail equality of distribution. Actual distributions depend on the necessary conditions for the achievement of equal rights. Often unequal distributions are a necessary condition for the achievement of equal rights. Vlastos's police-protection example illustrates this point exactly. What is important for Vlastos is not equal distributions, but rather the provision for equal rights.

The egalitarian positions which constitute the remainder of our discussion emphasize equal rights. Actual distributions are completely dependent on the achievement of equal rights. In each case, equality functions in conjunction with some other value and hence the positions are not purely egalitarian.

With these distinctions in mind, E_4 can be stated as follows:

E_4:   There are certain values to which men have an equal right. If some commodity a is a necessary condition for the achievement of some value y, then a should be distributed so that the equal right to y is achieved.

The determination of those values to which men have an equal right lies beyond the scope of this book. I shall assume that the following two equality principles are justified and hence *prima facie* are legitimate principles upon which to base specific distributions.

R_1: All men have an equal right to well-being.

R_2: All men have an equal right to liberty so long as it does not infringe upon the liberty of others.

If we accept R_1 and R_2, well-being and liberty can be substituted for y in E_4. In this way, R_1 and R_2 function within E_4 to determine the specific distribution of various commodities. If men have an equal right to well-being and if commodities $a \ldots n$ are necessary conditions for well-being, then men have an equal right to $a \ldots n$. However, in most cases, E_4 is not achieved by equal distribution. Suppose that S and T have an equal right to y and S needs a to achieve y while T needs b to achieve y. In this case, the egalitarian formula E_4 would instruct us to distribute a to S and b to T. We would not divide a and b equally between S and T. Moreover, E_4 commits us to distribute 100 units of c to S and 200 units of c to T, if those unequal amounts are necessary for the achievement of the equal rights of S and T. There is no set formula for actual distributions.

Objections. In spite of the conceptual clarity and explicit assumptions of E_4, the principle is not immune from philosophical criticism. The principle is subject to variations of the all-or-nothing counterexamples which proved so disastrous to E_3. Consider the following situation: If S and T's equal claim to y is to be met, then S should receive 100 units of a and T should receive 200 units. Unfortunately, there are only 225 units of a available for distribution. Given that S and T have an equal right to y, how should the 225 units be distributed? If the supply of commodities necessary for the achievement of equal rights is scarce, E_4 supplies no principle of distribution in these cases. It is one thing to assert that all men have an equal right to well-being or happiness; it is quite another to provide for that right. Conditions of scarcity always present problems for egalitarian theories.

It might appear that the egalitarian would have a ready answer to this objection. He might suggest that in conditions of scarcity the same ratio be applied as in conditions of adequacy. Hence if T receives twice as much as S when there are 300 units, he should also receive twice as much when there are 225 units. On this principle the just distribution of the 225 units would be to give 75 units to S and 150 units to T. Conditions of scarcity may alter the amount distributed, but it does not alter the ratio of distribution.

However, such an answer will not do. It is incorrect to say that the just ratio for distribution in conditions of plenty is also the just distribution in conditions of scarcity. Any commodity which is necessary for biological survival can be readily utilized to demonstrate this point. Suppose that S needs 100 units of food and T needs 200 units to achieve an equal right to well-being. However, both men need 80 units to keep alive. If the supply of food is limited to 225 units and the 2 to 1 ratio is maintained, S would starve to death. Food is at least one commodity where individual differences in taste can only be considered after each person has received at least a minimum share. What is true for food is true for most commodities. The ratios must be changed in conditions of scarcity. It is just common sense to realize that in conditions of plenty one may cater to individual tastes, but that in conditions of scarcity one ought not. If E_4 is to be an adequate principle of distributive justice, it must be amended to apply in conditions of relative scarcity.

A source of conflict. Another source of difficulty lies in possible conflicts between the equality principles. To distribute goods so that everyone's right to equality of well-being is achieved, is to distribute commodities in one way. The preservation of everyone's equality of freedom might require a different distribution of the same commodities. Such conflicts are rather common. In a free-enterprise system the consumer is considered sovereign. He can spend his income as he sees fit. This consumer sovereignty is justified by the principle of an equal right to freedom. On the other hand, it is also an accepted ethical principle that everyone has an equal right to a minimum standard of living even if he cannot earn the wages required for it. All nonvoluntary programs to achieve a certain equal minimum standard of living conflict with the principle of equal freedom. The wage-earner is not free to spend a certain amount of his income as he sees fit, but instead he is forced to subsidize the poor. The equal right to well-being conflicts with the equal right to freedom. The more equality principles a society accepts, the greater the possibility of conflict among them.

This discussion leads us to conclude that E_4 as stated would apply only in the following very limited case:

E_4 would apply only if the supply of goods is sufficient for the equal right to y to be achieved and if no conflict results by substituting some other value for y.

If the egalitarian is to provide a comprehensive and hence adequate theory of distributive justice, he must supply an egalitarian principle which is not limited to the special case. The remaining two sections of this chapter discuss this problem. Hence all the points of this section are still open for discussion in the following sections.

5. A Plausible Egalitarian Position

When E_4 cannot be applied, the egalitarian usually appeals to a limited principle of well-being. In scarcity situations, commodities should first be distributed so that a minimum standard of living is achieved by all. This can be formalized as E_5.

E_5: Everyone has an equal right to a minimum standard of living. All commodities should be distributed so that this equal right is obtained.

The position stated. Utilizing principles E_4 and E_5, a limited, but complete egalitarian position can be presented. I assume that this is the most plausible egalitarian position for distributive justice. If this position is inadequate, we should conclude that egalitarianism cannot provide an adequate theory of distributive justice. This egalitarian position has four points:

1. Up to some point p, commodities should be distributed so that a minimum standard of living is possible. Such a distribution is justified by the principle of an equal right to a minimum standard of living. (E_5)
2. After that point p, commodities should be distributed according to E_4. That is, commodities should be distributed so that equal rights to certain values, as expressed in accepted egalitarian principles, are achieved.
3. The point p is that point where the transition from E_5 to E_4 takes place, and this point of transition varies with circumstances.
4. Any distribution justified by one interpretation of y in E_4 must also be justified by any other interpretation of y where such interpretations result from accepted equality principles. The applications of accepted equality principles cannot justify conflicting distributions in the same situation.

This four-point egalitarian position has several advantages. First, it provides a theory which is relatively clear and precise, but which is not open to obvious counterexamples. Secondly, the theory is sufficiently comprehensive. Thirdly, the theory is sufficiently complex. It can deal with the sophisticated and complicated issues of distributive justice. E_5 provides a principle of priority, while E_4 can provide for great variety. Since there is no limit to the number of accepted equality principles, there is no limit to the number of values that can be accommodated.

6. Further Problems for Egalitarianism

Well-being. The first difficulty for the egalitarian position is a problem of specification and application. In this section we shall limit our discussion to the principle of an equal right to well-being (R_1). The principle of an equal right to liberty (R_2) will be discussed in Section 7. What does it mean to say that everyone has an equal right to well-being? In E_5, this principle is limited to an equal right to a minimum standard of living, where the minimum standard is determined on the basis of certain "basic needs." Although we shall discuss the relation of need and well-being in Chapter IV, we can conclude here that the criteria for a minimum standard of living depend on the state of the economy in question. Once you move beyond strictly biological needs, what is considered a basic need varies from society to society. It seems that E_5 is a cultural variant; a minimum standard of living, and hence the just distribution of commodities, varies from culture to culture.

More serious difficulties erupt when the principle of an equal right to well-being is not limited to a minimum standard of living. To expand the principle beyond the minimum is to present a dilemma. On the one hand, the age of affluence seems to demand that one's right to well-being extend beyond satisfaction of basic needs. If there is affluence, it seems that everyone has a right to at least some share of it. On the other hand, once the principle is extended, it becomes almost impossible to define adequately an equal right to well-being. There are several reasons for this. Suppose that we interpret the right in the broadest possible sense; everyone has an equal right to complete well-being. By complete well-being I mean maximum possible happiness. Hence, everyone has a right to maximum possible happiness. This interpretation of the principle of an equal right to well-being is subject to the following difficulties: First, it is impossible to achieve maximum possible happiness. Even in the most affluent societies, new demands are created so that there are never enough goods and services to go around. Hence maximum possible happiness cannot be achieved. Complete well-being is an ever-changing ideal. It expands without apparent limit. For this reason it could hardly function as a stable basis for a formula of distributive justice. Secondly, complete well-being is a function of an almost indefinite number of commodities. Moreover, the set of commodities which provide complete well-being for each individual is different in every case. The first task would be to classify commodities into general categories such as food, recreation, health care, etc. The second task would be to determine the amount from each category which each person requires for complete well-being. Both these tasks are, as a matter of practice, impossible. They are made impossible by individual variability and by the complex relationships involved. Even if these practical difficulties could be overcome, the provisions for complete well-being would likely violate other equal rights, especially the equal right to liberty. Finally, the equal right to complete well-being is an empty right. If everyone could satisfy all his desires, there would be no problem of distributive justice. Problems of distribution exist because our desires exceed our means for satisfying them. To argue that we should distribute so that an equal right to complete well-being is achieved is rather useless advice.

On the basis of this discussion, one can conclude that one's equal right to well-being lies somewhere between a minimum standard of living and complete well-being. However, the location of this "somewhere" is undetermined in egalitarian literature. The absence of egalitarian discussion on this point is probably a function of two factors. First, the nature of the problem has not been clearly recognized. Secondly, there seems to be no egalitarian basis on which it can be resolved. It is not a problem which admits of an egalitarian solution. The egalitarian position is inadequately specified and practicably impossible to apply.

Another difficulty. A second difficulty occurs at the transition point p when the egalitarian moves from E_5 to E_4. In those situations where scarcity prevents the application of E_4, it seems that the following rule for distribution is implied by the egalitarian position.

Given that scarcity blocks the direct application of E_4:
a. distribute the commodities in question so that a minimum standard of living is achieved
b. and then, distribute the remainder according to E_4.

This strategy is unsuccessful. We can illustrate this by considering our food example again. T is a gourmet; S is not. Hence, we shall assume that on the principle of an equal right to well-being, T should have 200 units of food, while S needs only 100. Unfortunately, there are only 226 units of food available for distribution. This scarcity situation would block the direct application of E_4 and require the adoption of the rule above. If each needs 80 units to stay alive, the rule above might provide two possibilities. If the rule is interpreted to mean that the remainder is to be distributed according to the ratio which would apply if the scarcity had not existed, then the distribution would be as follows:

S	80 plus 22	for a total of 102
T	80 plus 44	for a total of 124

In this case, S would have more than enough for well-being, while T would remain far below the level of well-being. The results of this distribution are clearly unjust.

One might amend part (b) of the rule above, however:

b.   then distribute the remainder according to the ratio which would
apply if scarcity had not existed so long as no one receives more
than he needs to achieve value *y* while another receives less.

The distribution could then be made as follows:

S	80 plus 20	for a total of 100
T	80 plus 46	for a total of 126

Although the distribution above would certainly conform to the rule, the distribution is unjust. In this case there is no reason why S should achieve well-being while T remains far below his well-being. Once conditions of scarcity block the direct application of E_4, there seems to be no point *p* where a transition to E_4 can take place. If it is necessary to invoke E_5, E_4 cannot be invoked to distribute the remainder. The egalitarian must find some other principle for distributing the remainder. When the supply of commodities is too scarce for the achievement of an equal right to well-being, but too plentiful for an equal right to a minimum standard of living, what egalitarian principle should apply? Neither E_4 nor E_5 nor E_4 and E_5 in conjunction is adequate. The only possible candidate is the formal E_3. To adopt E_3 however, would be to admit that in these situations, equality is a purely formal value and not a material one. This would weaken the egalitarian position considerably. There simply is no easy transition point from which we can move from one egalitarian formula to another or if there is, it does not appear in the egalitarian literature. However, the previous analysis had indicated that no one egalitarian formula can apply to all distributive situations. Problems of comprehensiveness still plague the egalitarian position.

Finally, the egalitarian position cannot resolve the all-or-nothing situations represented by the ice-floe example in Section 3. In these cases, any attempt to achieve even an equal right to minimum well-being is inadequate. Such an attempt would seal the doom of all. In such situations, the principle of an equal right to well-being is inadequate on any interpretation.

The discussion above clearly presents a serious challenge to the egalitarian position. A discussion of conflicting equality principles should make the challenge overwhelming.

7. Liberty and Equality

Conflicts may result in E_4 when more than one equality principle is acceptable. If the egalitarian is to take adequate account of the many values which must be considered in distributive justice, I assume that at least the two equality principles R_1 and R_2 (p. 61) are acceptable.

R_1: All men have an equal right to well-being.
R_2: All men have an equal right to liberty so long as it does not infringe upon the liberty of others.

Hence, well-being and liberty are acceptable interpretations of y in E_4. If the egalitarian position is adequate, any distribution justified by substituting well-being must also be justified by substituting liberty. If this condition is not met, R_1 and R_2 are in conflict.

The problem illustrated. Social security has been chosen as a commodity to illustrate how such conflicts result and how the egalitarian might circumvent them. With this discussion, we focus attention on what is inaccurately called the conflict between equality and liberty. At the outset, it must be emphasized that this conflict can occur at two levels.

1. Although a given distribution may be justified by both R_1 and R_2, the method of distribution violates R_2.
2. A distribution which is justified by the principle of an equal right to well-being violates the principle of an equal right to freedom.

Both in theory and in practice much of the discussion is focused on the first level. Usually the issue is one of government control. Although the role of government is always an important political question, it usually need not be an issue in moral disputes about distributive justice. If the sole reason for the dispute is whether some government agency should carry out the distribution, the egalitarian could usually avoid the issue by changing the method of distribution. The problem of government administration does not present a problem to the logic of the egalitarian position; it does not show that two equality principles justify contradictory distributions. It is extremely important to keep the logical issue distinct from the political issue. Such distinctions are necessary if we are to deal adequately with objections to the egalitarian position. Consider, for example, Milton Friedman's objection to social security:

> The citizen of the United States who is compelled by law to devote something like 10% of his income to the purchase of a particular kind of retirement contract administered by the government is being deprived of a corresponding part of his personal freedom.[16]

Friedman's objection cuts at both levels. In the first place he claims that

16. Milton Friedman, *Capitalism and Freedom* (Chicago: University of Chicago Press, 1962), p. 8.

the government monopoly is a violation of freedom. Since there are no competing social security plans, the social security system is in fact a nationalized industry. Friedman insists that a variety of plans be offered so that freedom of choice is protected. If we set aside some economic issues, philosophically Friedman's point can be granted. The egalitarian could support the competitive system which Friedman recommends. Although the egalitarians are usually portrayed as favoring programs instituted by the federal government, this attitude is not a logical implication of the egalitarian position. An egalitarian may quite consistently be a Jeffersonian on the political issue. The philosophical question at the first level only arises when a service can be distributed only by the federal government and when at least one person would choose to go without the service rather than accept government distribution. In this case the issue is whether the increase in well-being is worth the decrease in consumer freedom. This type of objection can be more effectively reformulated at the second level without any reference to a government program.

At the second level, the egalitarian position rests on two assumptions which I shall consider to be true.

1. It is technically impossible that social security work on a voluntary basis.
2. Social security is a necessary condition for the achievement of an equal right to well-being, and the society can afford such a program.

Friedman's objection is that such a program is clearly contrary to the principle of equality of freedom. If a person does not want to make provision for his old age, then that is up to him. He should not be compelled to do what others think to be in his best interest.

> Those of us who believe in freedom must believe also in the freedom of individuals to make their own mistakes. If a man knowingly prefers to live for today, to use his resources for current enjoyment, deliberately choosing a penurious old age, by what right do we prevent him from doing so?[17]

The egalitarian's answer is clear-cut. The equal right to a minimum standard of well-being justifies the loss of freedom to make a mistake. In this case a man must be deprived of his equal right to freedom so that others may achieve their equal right to a minimum standard of living.

An important digression. At this point, the egalitarian critic could salvage an important point. Conflicts between egalitarian principles can and do occur. Even if the loss of freedom is justified, the reality of the conflict does not

17. *Ibid.,* p. 188.

disappear. Unfortunately the typical response is not a criticism of the inconsistency of the egalitarian principles but rather an attack on egalitarian uniformity. It requires a brief digression to state this argument and to show its irrelevancy. Friedman's position is typical.

> Government can never duplicate the variety and diversity of individual action. At any moment in time, by imposing uniform standards in housing, nutrition, or clothing, government could undoubtedly improve the level of living by many individuals; by imposing uniform standards in schooling, road construction, or sanitation, central government could undoubtedly improve the level of performance in many local areas and perhaps even on the average of all communities. But in the process government would replace progress by stagnation; it would substitute uniform mediocrity for the variety essential for that experimentation which can bring tomorrow's laggards above today's mean.[18]

One could take issue with Friedman on factual grounds. Recent work by egalitarian welfare economists has provided strong arguments to show that it is the classical libertarian position which leads to uniformity and mediocrity. Specifically, the libertarian concept of consumer sovereignty is at fault. Individual liberty in the marketplace does not lead to diversity but instead to a dull uniformity of substandard goods. The argument is as follows:

1. The economic situation is such that most companies must operate at a high volume.
2. Since companies operate at a high volume, it is the tastes of the vast majority which are most important.
3. The tastes of the minority are either omitted or molded into the majority through advertising.
4. In any case, the minority tastes have little influence in the marketplace.
5. The informed and cultivated are in the minority.
6. Therefore the informed and cultivated lose influence.
7. This loss of influence is reflected in substandard products of a uniform nature designed for mass mediocrity.[19]

This is the form of argument used by those who criticize the mediocrity of the mass media, especially radio and television, and who support tax-supported FM radio and educational television. The argument is not without

18. *Ibid.,* p. 4.
19. This is a concise statement of arguments found in Tibor Scitovsky, "A Critique of Present and Proposed Standards" and "On the Principle of Consumer's Sovereignty" in *Papers on Welfare and Growth* (Stanford: Stanford University Press, 1964), pp. 232–40, 241–9.

merit and presents a serious challenge to the libertarian view of freedom based on consumer sovereignty.

However, even if no counterargument were forthcoming, Friedman's analysis completely distorts the issue. He unfairly attempts to burden the egalitarian with the onus of uniformity and mediocrity. However, the egalitarian position developed on the basis of E_4 and E_5 cannot be so burdened. I have shown conclusively that the equal right to well-being in no way entails sameness or uniformity. Even in conditions of scarcity where goods are distributed so as to achieve a minimum standard of living, there is little uniformity. The distributions still depend on individual need.

The real issue. The real question is not one of sameness but one of the use of coercion to provide a certain standard of living for others. It is this position which highlights the conflict.

> I find it hard as a liberal to see any justification for graduated taxation solely to redistribute income. This seems a clear case of using coercion to take from some in order to give to others and thus to conflict head on with individual freedom.[20]

This criticism challenges effectively the egalitarian position. Because the equality principles come into conflict, the basic problem of distributive justice cannot be resolved. The value conflicts cannot be eliminated. Moreover, any attempt to elevate the principle of equality of well-being, as egalitarians usually do, would generate numerous counterexamples. What is to have priority, equality of well-being or equality of freedom?

To avoid this difficulty, the egalitarian must make a two-step response. First he must show that he and his critic have different conceptions of freedom. Then he must show both the superiority of his own concept and its compatibility with a principle of an equal right to well-being.

One view of liberty. Libertarians like Friedman and Hayek understand freedom as freedom from political coercion. Freedom from the coercive actions of our fellow men is the most important freedom, and it is the only type of freedom which society can safely provide. It is worth quoting this position at length.

> [originally freedom] . . . meant freedom from arbitrary power of other men, release from the ties which left the individual no choice but obedience to the order of a superior to whom he was attached. The new freedom promised, however, was to be freedom from necessity, release from the compulsion of the circumstances which inevitably limit the range of choice

20. Friedman, *op. cit.,* p. 174.

for all of us, although for some more than others. . . . we used to be creative with what we have. We now wish to do away with these forces and to replace them by collective and conscious direction.[21]

As liberals, we take freedom of the individual, or perhaps the family, as our ultimate goal in judging social arrangements. Freedom as a value in this sense has to do with interrelations among people; it has no meaning whatsoever to a Robinson Crusoe on an isolated island. Robinson Crusoe on his island is subject to "constraint"; he has limited powers and he has only a limited number of alternatives, but there is no problem of freedom in the sense that is relevant to our discussion. . . . Political freedom means the absence of coercion of a man by his fellow men. The fundamental threat to freedom is power to coerce.[22]

The view of freedom which underlies these quotations can be formalized as follows:

L_1: S is free to do x only if S does x without being coerced by some other agent S'.

A man has liberty when he is free from the coercion of his fellow men.

If matters are left here, this view of freedom is paradoxical indeed. For on this view, it is irrelevant to speak of freeing a baseball player from the conditions which make him a weak hitter. We should only be concerned with freeing him from a government agency which places limitations on his contract. It is dangerous to speak of freeing an individual from ignorance, but not to speak of freeing him from compulsory membership in a labor union. It is foolhardy to free a person from the fear of accident and disability, but wise to free him from compulsory payments to retirement insurance.

This type of sarcastic criticism is possible because the L_1 libertarian has ignored all forms of coercion except the coercion of man over man. Completely omitted is consideration of the coercion of the environment, both internal and external. If the L_1 libertarian position is to be plausible, it must justify this limitation. The general argument is that an attempt to provide freedom from the environment leads to a loss of freedom from our fellow men. To free men from the conditions of the environment would make them a slave to other men. The argument for this position is as follows:

1. When men are coerced by the environment, they can be set free only by concentrated planning. For example, freedom from the business

21. Friedrich Hayek, *The Road to Serfdom* (Chicago: University of Chicago Press, 1944), pp. 25–6.
22. Friedman, *op. cit.*, pp. 12, 15.

cycle would entail government planning and intervention into the economy.

2. If the planning agency is to free us from the environment, it must control those factors which affect it. If the government is to control the business cycle, it must have some control over the interest rate, economic growth, unemployment, etc.

3. Although men usually desire the planning for the overall goal, they resent the loss of freedom with respect to the factors affecting the goal. No one wants a business cycle, yet some resent the loss of freedom to borrow money at the competitive rate.

4. However, such loss of freedom over the individual factors is necessary if the desired goal is to be achieved.

5. Therefore, attempts to free ourselves from natural constraints lead to a loss of political freedom.[23]

For this reason environmental coercion is omitted from the L_1 formula. To attempt to overcome environmental coercion is to threaten the political freedom we now have.

Negative and positive harm. Another attempt to make L_1 more plausible is to make a distinction between negative and positive harm. If this distinction is made, some of the alleged evils of an L_1 position are not evils at all. Only the alleged cures are evils.

The proponents of FEPC (Fair Employment Practice Commission) argue that interference with the freedom of individuals to enter into contracts with one another with respect to employment is justified because the individual who refuses to hire a Negro instead of a white, when both are equally qualified in terms of physical productive capacity, is harming others, namely, the particular color or religious group whose employment opportunity is limited in the process. This argument involves a very serious confusion between two very different kinds of harm. One kind is the positive harm that an individual does another by physical force, or by forcing him to enter a contract without his consent. . . . The second kind is the negative harm that occurs when individuals are unable to find mutually acceptable contracts, as when I am unwilling to buy something that someone wants to sell me and therefore make him worse off than he would be if I bought the item. . . . There is a strong case for using government to prevent imposing positive harm, which is to say, to prevent coercion. There is no case whatsoever for using the government to avoid the nega-

23. The basis for this argument is Hayek's *The Road to Serfdom.* See esp. chaps. 4 and 5.

tive kind of harm. On the contrary, such government intervention reduces freedom and limits voluntary cooperation.[24]

The thrust of this argument is to insist that we not confuse our strongly felt tastes with principles. There is no difference in principle between preferring a white to a Negro and preferring a classical singer to a popular one. We simply are repulsed by the former taste. However, the appropriate strategy is to try to persuade others; it is not to force our tastes on them.[25] To elevate differences in taste into differences in principle is to threaten freedom; it threatens to impose the tastes of the majority on the minority.

The egalitarian view of freedom. The egalitarian challenges the L_1 libertarian on every point. First, he provides an alternative account of liberty which is enhanced, not destroyed, by his egalitarian position. On his view,

L_2: S is free to do x at t
    if and only if
  (1) S has the ability to do x at t
  (2) if there is some alternative y such that
      (a) S has the ability to do y at t
      (b) S knows of the opportunity to do y at t
      (c) y would also enable S to achieve his purpose if he wanted to do it
      (d) no other agents' coerces S to do x instead of y.

L_2 is far more complicated than L_1. For L_2 it is not sufficient that no second party limits the alternatives for a man to be free. A man is not free unless he has genuine alternatives, that is, unless he has alternative means to achieve his purposes and has the power to act on them. Genuine alternatives, knowledge of these alternatives, and the ability to act on them are the necessary conditions of freedom.

Secondly, the egalitarian criticizes the L_1 libertarian for failing to take these necessary conditions into account. The types of coercion they overlook are those which must be eliminated if the freedom they desire is possible. If political freedom is to be achieved, men must have control of their economic and social destinies as well. An unskilled laborer does not have control over the economic aspect of his life when a lack of education confines him to a dirty, smelly, low-paying job. There is ample empirical evidence that a full stomach is more highly valued than the right to vote. Freedom from want and freedom from ignorance are necessary conditions for political freedom.

24. Friedman, *op. cit.,* p. 113.
25. *Ibid.,* p. 111.

Thirdly, the egalitarian takes strong exception to the distinction between positive and negative harm. One might admit that there is a metaphysical difference between coercion and discrimination, but often there is no ethical difference. What is the ethical difference between stealing $100 from a Negro and paying him $100 less for a job simply because he is a Negro? There is a metaphysical difference between physical coercion and taking advantage of another's ignorance. However, what is the ethical difference between stealing and utilizing a consumer's ignorance to sell him a shoddy product, disguise the true rate of interest, or beguiling him into a disadvantageous contract? Justice does not depend on metaphysical distinctions between acts as forced or unforced, but rather it depends on moral distinctions. In certain situations it is immoral to act on our tastes even if we are free to do so. In these cases the exercise of freedom would be a moral abuse of freedom. Libertarians like Friedman have been unjustified in elevating a metaphysical distinction into a moral distinction.

Having undermined the L_1 position, the egalitarian would then attempt to demonstrate the compatibility between freedom and equality, that is, between the principle of an equal right to well-being and an equal right to liberty (L_2). The egalitarian may argue that if L_2 is to be achieved, society has the responsibility to provide the necessary conditions for freedom where they are absent. Where there is ignorance, society ought to provide education. If there is unemployment society should provide jobs. It is the duty of society to remove those limitations of the environment which eliminate alternatives for self-development. Because men have an equal right to liberty$_2$, they have an equal right to well-being. An equal right to well-being is a necessary condition for an equal right to liberty$_2$. The equality principles, when properly understood, are perfectly compatible.

The remaining conflict. In political and social philosophy, the issue discussed above is most crucial. Unfortunately labels such as liberal, conservative, capitalist, socialist, welfare statist, have obscured the logical issues. Although the discussion above is extremely limited,[26] it is hoped that the two positions are clearly presented and that the logical issues between them are sharply drawn. In particular, it is hoped that the use of "liberty" or "freedom" by both positions is clear. If these hopes have been realized, we can apply the results of this digression to our analysis of the egalitarian position.

26. The most important omission is the recent work in the paradox of obtaining social decisions from individual decisions. This has been omitted because the method of this paper is prescriptive and hence avoids these difficulties. However, the interested reader should see Kenneth Arrow, *Social Choice and Individual Values,* 2nd ed. (New York: John Wiley & Sons, Inc., 1963). This edition takes account of recent criticisms and refers the reader to other sources of information.

Although the egalitarian–L_2 libertarian alliance may provide a plausible and consistent theory, it cannot be used exclusively as a principle of distributive justice. The conflicts between this principle and others remain. We may speak of the conflict in terms of a conflict between the principle of an equal right to well-being and an equal right to freedom or we may now speak of the conflict as one between two different conceptions of freedom. Whatever the semantics, the conflict remains real. Sometimes one must take from T in order to give education, health care, etc. to S. This might be done to achieve an equal right to well-being or an equal right to liberty. However, it is always open to T to protest that his equal right to well-being or freedom is being violated. In some cases an egalitarian may justly deprive T to provide for S. In other cases he may not. The problem for the egalitarian is that he can provide no further principle for resolving these conflicts. His opponent can often present a case which either (a) uses the same egalitarian principle to defend his own position or (b) can appeal to a nonegalitarian principle which he believes has priority in this situation. The considerations of Sections 6 and 7 lead to the conclusion that the egalitarian position based on E_4 and E_5 is not adequate as a theory of distributive justice.

8. Conclusion

Although our search for an adequate egalitarian formula of distributive justice has been in vain, some important insights into the problem of distributive justice have been achieved.

First, I conclude that usually there is no moral reason for an equal distribution per se. Equal distribution is not a value in itself. Equality is not an independent value, but always functions with some other value. If a distribution is equal, it is because men are equal in some respect which is relevant to that distribution. This conclusion is supported by the demonstrated inadequacies of E_1 and E_2 and by the analysis of E_3, E_4, and E_5.

Secondly, I conclude that there is no need to base an egalitarian position on the equal distribution of commodities. E_4 and E_5 are illustrations of egalitarian positions which utilize equality principles to determine distributions. However, the equality principles in no way entail equal distributions. This type of position enables the egalitarian to avoid the traditional criticisms of sameness and mediocrity.

Thirdly, I conclude that the inadequacies of the egalitarian formulas and combinations of formulas follow a certain pattern. This pattern has already appeared in the analysis of utilitarianism. The first difficulty is to state the position clearly and to specify the meaning of the terms. Secondly, there are practical problems of application. It is difficult to know when E_5 should be replaced by E_4. Finally, the formulas are too limited. They cannot accommodate the many values which must be considered if distributive justice is to be done. This limitation makes the formula vulnerable to counterexamples. In each case, the strategy of the counterexample is to present a situation in which some other value has priority over the egalitarian formula in that case. As with utilitarianism, an adequate statement of the position will provide a good deal of the mileage in the search for an adequate theory of distributive justice. However, the egalitarian position is not sufficient to enable us to complete the journey.

IV. A Socialist Formula of Distributive Justice

THE INADEQUACIES of the utilitarian and egalitarian theories require that we resume our search for an adequate theory of distributive justice. In this chapter we focus our attention on the so-called socialist formula which can be formulated as follows:

> S: A just distributive system is one in which everyone produces according to his ability and receives according to his need.

This formula is attributed to the French socialist, Louis Blanc. It is one element of the German socialists' Gotha Program of 1875 and is apparently accepted as the distributive principle in the final stage of communism by both Marx and Lenin.[1]

In point of fact, the formula above cannot be referred to as the socialist formula without considerable qualification. "Socialism" is given such a wide-ranging application that there is no one formula of distributive justice common to all so-called socialist positions. Moreover, one seldom finds one socialist position that adheres to one formula in all situations. Hence, historically speaking there is no warrant for speaking of *the* socialist position.

To avoid relying on one formula as a principle of distributive justice is a sound strategy. In this respect, the flexibility of many socialist positions is correct. Unfortunately, however, socialists are notoriously unclear as to what particular principles of distribution they accept and under what conditions each of them applies. As we shall see they carelessly relate equal distribution, distribution according to need, and distribution according to work. This

---

1. The Gotha text and the comments by Marx and Lenin can be found in Karl Marx, *Critique of the Gotha Program* (London: Lawrence and Wishart, Limited, 1938). Marx's comments are from his *Critique of the Gotha Program,* p. 14. Lenin's comments are from his notebook "Marxism on the State," pp. 76–7. The Gotha Program reference is found on p. 107.

tendency is extremely confusing at best and inconsistent and contradictory at worst. Moreover, even when the various principles are distinguished from one another, they are inadequately applied.

Given the situation described above, my strategy with respect to socialism is as follows: The bulk of the chapter is concerned with an analysis and criticism of the principle, "from each according to his ability, to each according to his need." I shall refer to this principle as the socialist formula and I shall refer to any adherent of it as a socialist. By concentrating on this formula, I am obviously not concerned with orthodox Marxism since it is clear that Marx intended the socialist formula to apply only in the final stages of communism. Historically, my remarks are most relevant to the English and French socialism of the non-Marxist tradition. It is especially akin to that socialist philosophy which stretches from early French communist thinkers to the welfare state principles of Beveridge.

Unfortunately, however, it is just this non-Marxist French and English socialist tradition where great confusion between equal distribution and distribution according to need is a commonplace. As I have already indicated in Chapter III, equal distribution and distribution according to need must be kept separate. Hence, I shall simplify the traditional position by considering only the principle of distribution according to need. This simplification is necessary in order to concentrate on the strengths and weaknesses of the need formula as a principle of distributive justice. This simplification is justified by the conceptual clarity and precision which are gained. Should anyone feel that my criticisms of the need formula can be resolved by appealing to the principle of equal distribution, he is invited to turn again to my discussion of equal distribution in Chapter III.

With this emphasis in mind, I have organized the chapter in the following way. In Section 1, I address myself to the difficulties of socialism in general. Various socialist positions are distinguished and criticized. The basic thrust of the criticisms is to show that the positions either confuse several principles of distribution or that they ignore the problem of distribution. The remaining sections are limited to the formula "from each according to his ability, to each according to his need." In Section 2, the formula will be amplified and explained. Sections 3 to 5 are critical in nature. In Section 3 the discussion will be focused on the conceptual clarity of the formula. In Section 4 the issue of practicability will be considered. Finally, in Section 5 various counterexamples to the socialist formula will be presented. The strategy of the counterexamples will be identical to that used in Chapters II and III. In this case it will be shown that values omitted by the socialist formula are relevant values to be applied in certain circumstances.

1. Socialist Positions—Sorting Issues and Criticisms

The Marxist tradition. Marx carefully distinguishes the socialist stage from the communist stage in economic development. Distribution according to need is reserved for the communist stage. However, since the bulk of Marx's analysis is concerned with the socialist stage of economic development, the need formula is relatively unimportant in his thought.

In the socialist stage of development, Marx believes that each should receive according to the value of his work. This principle should not be confused with the principle of distribution of utilitarian economics, "to each according to his marginal productivity." Marx believed that the worker did not receive an income equal to the full value of his labor. Instead the worker received an income which only provided for subsistence. The difference between the subsistence wage and a wage equal to the full value of labor was expropriated by the capitalists. This expropriation was possible because of the capitalist's monopoly of the means of production. The purpose of the socialist revolution is to seize the means of production, destroy the capitalist monopoly, and provide each worker the full value of his labor.

Even if we ignore the inadequacies of Marxian economics, the formula "to each according to his work" is inadequate as a principle of distributive justice. In the first place, it is doubtful that Marx intended the formula to be a principle of distributive justice. Marx's lack of concern with distributive justice has been persuasively discussed in an article by Robert Tucker whose point ". . . is simply that the common image of Marx as a prophet of social justice is a false one and that those who have seen distributive justice as the main moral issue of his Marxism have been mistaken."[2]

The following evidence for this view can be cited. Marx seemed to believe that notions of morality and justice are a function of the material conditions of society. The capitalist system of exploitation had developed by necessity. Marx viewed the moral condemnations of capitalism by other socialists as "unscientific." The capitalist system had to be understood, not condemned. Marx also did not share the ethical ideals of other socialists, especially the ideal of equality. Such attitudes expressed a "petit bourgeoise mentality." Marx's attitude is clearly seen in his attack on Proudhon in *The Poverty of Philosophy.*

In the second place, the formula "to each according to his work" is not sufficient to provide distributive justice. Since income would be solely a

2. Robert C. Tucker, "Marx and Distributive Justice" in *Nomos VI Justice,* ed. Carl Friedrich and John Chapman (New York: Atherton Press, 1963), pp. 309–10.

function of labor, such factors as health, family size, and other special needs would be omitted from consideration. Such factors must be considered, however, if the distribution of income is to be just.

Upon moving to the communist stage of economic development, Marx's principle of distribution according to need is virtually useless. The communist society is a society of abundance, and by "abundance" Marx seems to mean a society in which all needs can be provided. However, since satisfaction of all needs can be provided, the problem of distributive justice in such a society is a practical problem. The goods and services must be distributed to the right people. Hence, the practical problem is to make sure that the abundance is distributed so that the commodities match needs. "To each according to his need" is a practical principle. The two million aspirins must go to hospitals and not to prisons. However, "to each according to his need" is not a principle of distributive *justice*. One is unjust if he deprives another from fulfilling a basic need in order to satisfy a less urgent need of his own, but one is perverse if he keeps more than he needs and hence deliberately deprives others in a society of abundance. One can be immoral in a society of complete abundance. However, a principle of distributive justice which by definition is a principle for distributing goods and services in conditions of scarcity is not required.

In summary, the Marxist tradition cannot provide a theory of distributive justice. At the socialist stage of economic development, Marx did not intend the formula "to each according to his work" to be a principle of distributive justice. Moreover, it is not sufficient to provide distributive justice in any case. In the communist stage of economic development, the formula "to each according to his need" is virtually useless since there are no problems of distributive justice in a communist society.

Socialism and efficiency. Recently a group of socialists has attempted to show that a planned economy can meet the optimum conditions for efficiency discussed in Chapter II. In other words, these socialists argue that a planned socialist economy can provide maximum efficiency as well as, or better than, a competitive market economy.[3]

The resulting controversy between these socialists and their capitalist counterparts is not of concern here. What is of concern is the principle of dis-

3. See articles by Oskar Lange and Fred M. Taylor in *On the Economic Theory of Socialism,* ed. Benjamin E. Lippincott. (Minneapolis: University of Minnesota Press, 1938), pp. 41–129. See also Abba Lerner, *The Economics of Control* (New York: Macmillan Company, 1944) and Enrico Barone "The Ministry of Production in the Collectivist State" *Collectivist Economic Planning,* ed. F. A. Hayek (London: Routledge, 1935), pp. 245–90. Also Abram Bergson, "Socialist Economics" *Essays in Normative Economics* (Cambridge, Mass.: Harvard University Press, 1966), pp. 193–236.

tribution these socialists adopt. On the whole, distribution has not been widely discussed. In this respect, these socialists are at one with their opponents. However, Oscar Lange has provided a brief discussion in which he argues that socialism can maximize welfare better than a competitive market economy. In distribution two conditions will be observed.[4]

C_1: It will be assumed that the marginal utility of income is the same for all and that the same price offered by different consumers represents an equal urgency of need.

C_2: The distribution must lead to the apportionment of services of labor so that the value of marginal productivity equals the marginal disutility of pursuing the occupation.

As I understand them, these conditions affect distribution in the following way. According to C_1 if Smith and Jones are both willing to pay $10 for a radio, then their needs for the radio are equal, and $10 can be distributed to each. According to C_2, if Smith is an office clerk and Jones is a test pilot, we must pay more money to Jones because the disutility (danger) of being a test pilot far exceeds that of being a clerk.

In distribution, both C_1 and C_2 must be considered. In the example above, Smith would have to do with a cheaper radio, since Jones has a more dangerous job which should be compensated more highly than Smith's. In distribution, total utility should be equal.

This theory is not without difficulty, however. It is subject to all the problems of the measurement and comparison of utilities discussed in Chapter II. Moreover, it is not clear whether one should consider the utility of an occupation or the utility which an individual enjoys from pursuing that occupation. If we say that being a clerk has a higher utility than being a test pilot, instances of injustice can result. Suppose Jones despises desk jobs and is challenged by danger. If the income from clerical work and test piloting were equal, he would still choose the latter. Hence, it is not clear that he should receive more money for doing the work he most enjoys. On the other hand, if C_2 is interpreted to apply to the individual's utility with respect to a given job, other difficulties arise. Suppose Jones preferred to be a test pilot but he knew that no amount of extra money could induce the Smiths in the world to become test pilots. The Smiths enjoy being passengers but they have no desire whatsoever to be pilots. In such a situation, it is clear that Jones could receive an income greater than that which he would receive if his own desires for being a test pilot were the only consideration. Smith should probably pay something extra for his complete refusal to be a test pilot, but it is not clear that all the advantage should go to Jones. Since the C_2 principle is ambiguous, and since it is unlikely that

4. Lange, "On the Economic Theory of Socialism" in Lippincott ed., *op. cit.*, pp. 101–3.

C_1 and C_2 can harmoniously work together in all cases, it seems that this socialist utilitarian formula is not sufficient to provide distributive justice.

The French and English tradition. The principle of distribution "to each according to his need" is most prominent in the French and English socialist tradition. The French socialist Louis Blanc is given credit for the formula "from each according to his ability, to each according to his need." A distributive system based on need goes back at least as far as the French communist Morelly in his work, *Code of Nature* (1755).

> Someone who needs, for example, green vegetables, or fruits will go to the public square . . . and take what he needs for one day only. If someone needs bread, he will go to the baker and get the quantity that he needs for some specified period.[5]

Presently, this emphasis on need continues in English welfare state socialism where the urgent needs of all citizens are met from "the cradle to the grave."

Unfortunately, many socialists of this tradition either confuse distribution according to need with equal distribution or adopt several principles of distributive justice without specifying when each of them applies. Two illustrations of this tendency are given below.

> To be more specific, it is necessary to bind together everyone's lot . . . to assure to every man and his posterity no matter how numerous it may be, as much as they need, but no more than they need. . . . The sole means of arriving at this is to establish . . . a simple administration of needs, which keeping a record of all individuals and all the things that are available to them will distribute these available goods with the most scrupulous equality. . . . But the general Reformer would like to obtain for all individuals without distinction, an absolutely equal portion of all the goods and advantages that can be enjoyed in this mean world.[6]
>
> According to Cicero, no one has a right to more than he needs. . . . The doctrine of Cicero leads directly to equality.[7]

Quotations like those above could be produced almost indefinitely. Since I have already discussed the relation between production and distribution and have carefully distinguished distribution according to need and equal distribu-

5. Morelly, "Code of Nature" *Socialist Thought—A Documentary History,* ed. Albert Fried and Ronald Sanders (Garden City, N.Y.: Doubleday & Company, Inc., 1964), pp. 21-2.
6. "Gracchus" Babeuf, "Babeuf's Defense" and "Letter to Dubois de Fosseux" in Fried and Sanders ed., *op. cit.,* pp. 67-8, 46.
7. Pierre Joseph Proudhon, *What is Property* in Fried and Sanders ed., *op. cit.,* p. 213. Another somewhat involved example of this confusion is found in the same work, pp. 127-8.

tion, the remainder of this chapter will be limited to a discussion of Blanc's principle "from each according to his ability, to each according to his need." By concentrating on this aspect of the French and English socialist tradition, we shall avoid material previously discussed and be able to focus our attention on a formula of distribution according to need.

2. The Socialist Formula Explained

The first task is to place Blanc's socialist formula within the value framework of this book. In other words, what values do the socialists seek to realize in a just distributive system?

In production, the socialist cultivates the value of skill or ability. Each man should contribute to the productive task by utilizing his skills or abilities. Production is the means for the realization of human potentiality. In distribution, the socialist seeks to achieve happiness or well-being. This is why distribution is made according to need. Happiness is the result of need satisfaction. Hence, in the language of this book, the socialist formula can be restated as follows:

S: A just distributive system is one in which production is the realization of individual skill or ability and distribution is the realization of happiness in the satisfaction of one's needs.

Advantages of the socialist formula. Compared with previous formulas, the socialist formula is relatively clear and plausible. For example, the socialist formula specifies what happiness is: Happiness results from the satisfaction of needs. Moreover, the socialist formula has an initial intuitive appeal. There is no need to perform a series of reformulations at the outset to provide some degree of plausibility as was necessary with the egalitarian position. At the preanalytic level the socialist formula seems both clear and plausible.

The socialist formula is also highly specific and individual. A given distribution is not justified on the basis of an abstract value; it is justified in a specific situation on the basis of individual need. In this way, individual differences are taken into account and unrealistic classifications are avoided.

Finally, the socialist formula makes reference to production, which must be considered if one is to have an adequate theory of distributive justice. Hence, the formula makes reference to both production and distribution. Moreover, need and ability are not static concepts. The socialist formula will still apply as human needs and abilities change.

These advantages indicate that the socialist formula shows some promise as a candidate for an adequate theory of distributive justice. In the remaining sections, I will scrutinze the socialist formula to determine what objections can be raised against it and to see what extent these *prima facie* advantages can withstand the test of philosophical criticism.

---

3. The Conceptual Clarity of the Socialist Formula

If the preanalytic feeling of clarity and precision is to be justified, the central concepts of ability and need must be clearly understood.

The concept of ability. Unfortunately, there is no elaborate discussion of "ability" in the tradition of French and English socialism. In what follows I shall try to give a reasonable characterization of "ability" which is sufficiently adequate to overcome some standard objections.

A discussion of ability requires two levels. On the first level "ability" refers to the qualifications which one has for a given job. On the second level, "ability" refers to how well one performs within an occupation. I shall refer to these two levels of ability as $ability_1$ and $ability_2$.

On the first level, the socialist could say that one is producing according to his $ability_1$ when he is employed in the occupation for which he is fitted. It seems that fittingness would be determined in a manner similar to present guidance tests. A list of necessary skills and personal traits is drawn up for each occupation. Each person is then tested to see which skills and personal traits he possesses. A simple procedure matches the person's abilities with the correct occupation.

Once a person is employed, however, a second notion of ability is required. In this case, we must know if, on the job, a person is producing according to his $ability_2$. It seems that this knowledge would depend on the possibility of providing objective standards of productivity for each job. If such standards are possible, a person would be producing according to his $ability_2$ when he is producing according to the standard for his particular job. The obvious difficulty is to find an objective basis for the standards. Should there be a universal standard for each job or should there be several standards adjusted to the individual differences of the worker? The socialist would probably try to avoid this thorny issue by letting the requirements of the job "speak for themselves." If the requirements are such that it seems reasonable to believe that all those who have $ability_1$ for the job possess this ability equally, a universal standard for performance is perfectly satisfactory. If we cannot assume equality of ability$_1$, more specific standards will be required.

A difficulty. Unfortunately this conception of ability$_2$ is simply inappropriate for many occupations. Standards of productivity may make perfectly good sense when applied to industrial and clerical occupations; they make far less sense when applied to the professions and the arts. Physicians and sculptors are not producers the way farmers and auto assembly-line workers are. Standards of *productivity* are just not relevant in the former occupations. This criterion must be amended by omitting the reference to productivity. When so amended, one is working according to his ability$_2$ if he is meeting the appropriate standards for his occupation. This might eliminate the problem with the professions. A surgeon, for example, would be operating according to his ability$_2$ when the postoperative death rate of his patients is at or below the standard. Such an amendment would not eliminate the problem presented by the arts, however. The nature of the arts is such that standards are at best problematic. Artistic creativity is constantly breaking through them. You cannot determine whether an artist is performing according to his ability$_2$ by counting the works of art he produces or by judging the kinds of works he produces. An objective standard for measuring ability$_2$ seems inappropriate in the arts. In this area the proposed characterization of ability breaks down. However, it is unlikely that any socialist could give an adequate characterization of "from each according to his ability" when this aspect of the formula is applied to the arts. At best, any socialist formula would have limited application in this area.

On the whole, however, a person is working according to his ability when (a) he performs the job for which he is fitted, and (b) he performs according to the standard for his occupation.

The concept of need. Far more difficult than the provision of an adequate concept of ability is the provision of an adequate concept on need. The socialist formula is deceptively simple at this point. If the products necessary for need satisfaction were as abundant as sand, distribution according to need would present few problems. All nonconflicting needs could be satisfied. However, problems of distributive justice arise because not all needs can be satisfied; the necessary commodities are simply not available. It is silly to insist that distributions be made according to need when this clearly cannot be done. Needs must be arranged in a hierarchy according to priorities so that the most important needs will be satisfied first. Only if this is done will the socialist formula make any sense.

The socialists have attempted to surmount this objection by arguing that the claim to need fulfillment is proportionate to the urgency of the need. The needs related to biological survival and physical health take precedence over the others. For example the socialist L. T. Hobhouse has argued that since the need for food is more urgent than the need for beauty, need claims must be ranked according to their urgency.[8] The socialist formula must be reformulated as follows:

S':   A just distributive system is one in which everyone produces according to his ability and receives according to his need, where the claim to need is proportioned to urgency.

Basic needs. In general, a need is considered basic if it is a biological need necessary for survival or physical health. The fulfillment of basic needs is a necessary condition for the fulfillment of other needs. A basic need is a function of man's biological nature. Moreover, it is commonly believed that such needs can be determined with a fair degree of objectivity.[9] In addition, this notion of a basic need is also widely accepted in all distributive theories. Basic needs determine the welfare floor in utilitarian theories and the right to a minimum standard of living in egalitarian theories. To raise legitimate, but embarrassing, questions concerning the determination of basic needs is to pose difficulties for all the distributive theories considered thus far. Hence, I will grant the socialist the concept of basic need, and I will admit that basic needs are more urgent than others and that they should be satisfied first.

Nonbasic needs. Unfortunately, a distinction between basic and nonbasic needs is not sufficient for the socialist's purposes. This is established in the following simple argument:

1.   Most societies can provide for all basic needs.
2.   No society can provide for all nonbasic needs.
3.   Hence, the controversial distributive decisions occur at the level of nonbasic needs.
4.   Since not all nonbasic needs can be satisfied some criterion must be provided so that we know which nonbasic needs should be satisfied first.
5.   Hence, if the socialist formula is to apply, nonbasic needs must be ranked according to urgency.

This kind of problem results in any society beyond the subsistence level. Given that basic needs can be met and that not all other needs can be met, a socialist must make some decision about priorities. How is that decision to be made?

8. L. T. Hobhouse, *The Elements of Social Justice* (New York: Henry Holt and Company, 1922), p. 112.
9. Kenneth Arrow, *Social Choice and Individual Values,* 2nd ed. (New York: John Wiley & Sons, Inc., 1951), p. 87, and S. I. Benn and R. S. Peters, *The Principles of Political Thought* (New York: Collier Books, 1964), pp. 162-7.

What seems to be required is a characterization of nonbasic needs such that they can be ranked according to some criterion of urgency. If this could be done, the socialist would then have a means for applying his formula. The goods and services would be distributed until they are exhausted, the needs of first priority being satisfied first and those of lowest priority remaining unsatisfied. The difficulty, however, is to provide a characterization of nonbasic needs that will do the job.

Certainly, the socialist does not want to characterize nonbasic needs in terms of desire. This is easily seen when we consider the nature of the two following statements in which x does not refer to a basic need or desire:

1. S needs x.
2. S desires x

These statements are of different logical types. Since (2) is a report of S's psychological state, it makes no sense to ask if S really desires x when he says he does. In this respect statement (2) is incorrigible. Statement (1), on the other hand, is an entirely different kind of statement. It can make sense to ask S if he needs x when he says he does. S may feel that he needs x, but it still may be false that he needs x; in this respect statement (1) is corrigible. Moreover, a distribution based on (2) entails that the distribution be based on the desires of S. A distribution based on (1) does not entail that the distribution be based on the desires of S. S may desire what he needs, but again he may not. We shall mark this distinction by saying that (1) is objective and (2) is subjective. Hence, we are logically permitted to say that statements about nonbasic needs are objective in a way in which statements about desires are not.

Nonbasic needs and objectivity. In light of our discussion above, consider the following statement in which x refers to a nonbasic need: S needs x but T does not. What the socialist requires is a concept of nonbasic need such that the determination of the need can be made independently of the beliefs of S and T. Such statements about nonbasic needs should be objective in this sense. However, I maintain that many statements about nonbasic needs are not objective in this way. Consider the statements below:

1. Smith needs the blood plasma more than Jones.
2. Smith needs medicine more than Jones needs food.
3. Smith needs a holiday more than Jones.
4. Smith needs a holiday more than Jones needs to see a symphony.

Statements (1) and (2) are about basic needs and are objective in the sense required. For the socialist formula to work, statements (3) and (4) must be objective in the same way. Unfortunately there are good reasons to think they are not objective in this way. Statements (3) and (4) are different in more than degree from statements (1) and (2). The distinction between those needs which are reasonably determinate and hence objective and those needs which are not reasonably determinate and hence not objective has been elaborated by S. I. Benn and R. S. Peters in their book *The Principles of Political Thought.*[10] Some of the theoretical and practical problems which result when need is made the criterion of distributive justice can now be illustrated.

The problem of priorities. First, there is no objective way to mark priorities. The distinction between basic and nonbasic needs succeeded because the satisfaction of some needs is a necessary condition for the satisfaction of others. It seems clear that the whole range of nonbasic needs cannot be distinguished on the basis of this criterion. For example, we do not know, except for basic needs, what needs must be satisfied as a necessary condition for satisfying our aesthetic needs. Nor do we know that satisfying aesthetic needs is a necessary condition for satisfying other needs. In addition, there is often insufficient evidence for saying that some nonbasic needs are more urgent than others. Moreover, there is seldom conventional agreement that certain nonbasic needs are more essential than others. For these reasons it could not be a policy of distribution that dine-and-dance clubs are more important than symphony concerts or that additional public parks are more important than the undisturbed wilds of nature. Such a policy could be ruled out because one cannot say that the need for physical relaxation is more urgent than the need for aesthetic contemplation. Unlike basic needs, the urgency of many nonbasic needs is a matter of taste; neither science nor convention enables us to rank them uniformly.

The problem of need determination. Further difficulties arise when we ask who has nonbasic needs and whose nonbasic needs should be satisfied first. For example, de Jouvenel contends that college professors have a need to entertain their colleagues and students in a comfortable and cultured manner.[11] The nonbasic need is a result of the role which a professor plays. However, is the professor really different from anyone else? Everyone has a need to entertain his friends and associates. The professor is certainly not unique in this respect. Perhaps de Jouvenel's point is that the professor's need takes precedence over others in times of scarcity. If society lacks the commodities to allow everyone to entertain, then the professor's claim has priority over the others. However, this is not at all evident, since the professor's need to entertain his colleagues

10. Benn and Peters, *The Principles of Political Thought* (New York: Collier Books, 1964), pp. 162–70.
11. Bertrand de Jouvenel, *The Ethics of Redistribution* (Cambridge: Cambridge University Press, 1951), p. 54.

is no more important than a businessman's or a physician's. Nor does the professor's functional need have obvious priority over other nonbasic needs. A steel worker might argue that a weekly poker party satisfies his need for relaxation and that his need for relaxation has priority over the professor's functional need. Such a conflict would return us to the problem above. Hence, with many nonbasic needs one cannot accurately determine who has the need or compare the urgency of those who do.

Nonbasic needs and the means of fulfillment. De Jouvenel may have had another meaning for his contention. Perhaps he only wishes to assert that a professor has a need for more income because he has to entertain in a certain style The poker party will just not do. This raises a third difficulty; namely, that in many cases there is no basis for determining which commodities are genuinely needed to satisfy nonbasic needs. For any individual, we know how much medicine is necessary to cure the flu. However, we do not know which commodities are necessary to fulfill needs for relaxation. To use Benn and Peters' example we cannot know objectively whether Saturday nights at the movies are sufficient to satisfy our need for relaxation or whether a luxury cruise is required instead.[12]

One might appeal to an average. The distribution should be made according to what most people need to fulfill their nonbasic needs. If a trip to the cinema is sufficient on the average, the distribution should be based on that. However, such a position assumes that it is meaningful to speak of averages in such situations. For my part, I have no idea what such averages might be or how they should be discovered. Moreover, even if the determination of such averages were possible, distributions according to them would certainly not be just. Some would receive far more than they require; others would receive far less. A distribution which produces unnecessary waste on the one hand and unnecessary deprivation on the other is certainly not just.

At this point the socialist might appeal to the future development of the social sciences as a means for eliminating the difficulties presented above. Psychology may be able to provide considerable detail as to what needs are urgent and as to the amounts of goods and services various individuals require to fulfill their needs. Already, the urgency of the nonbasic needs for education, freedom from unemployment, and security against misfortune are fairly objectively established. These needs have precedence over other nonbasic needs. However, progress in this area is very slow, and for most nonbasic needs the problem of establishing objective priorities continues to be a real one. Moreover, there are many problems with the socialist formula which a more highly developed social science cannot resolve.

12. Benn and Peters, *op. cit.,* p. 168.

Shortages within need categories. Consider a situation in which all the secondary needs have been ranked according to urgency $N_1 \ldots N_n$. Moreover, for each need a priority list for individuals has been drawn up $S_1 \ldots S_n$. However, the supply of commodities is such that all secondary needs up through N_3 can be satisfied and at N_4 some of the needs of the group which has first priority (S_1) can be satisfied. Unfortunately not all of those in S_1 can be satisfied. On what basis shall the distribution be made? Clearly, the socialist formula must stand mute; it has nothing more to say in this case. No further distinctions on the basis of need are possible. However, the only possible distributions according to the socialist formula are distributions based on need. We have found an area where the socialist formula does not apply. Even with a comprehensive list of implausible need priorities, the socialist formula is too restrictive.

Need conflicts and morals. All the foregoing difficulties reappear when need conflicts are considered. Consider two rival farmers in a highly competitive situation. Each has a need to be successful. Both farmers would benefit from a new weed killer. Jones would use it to improve the productivity of his crops. Smith would use it to kill Jones. Although both men have a claim to the poison on the basis of need, it is clearly unjust to distribute it according to need.

The above example merely points out the obvious. Certain needs of the criminal, the mentally ill, the cruel, and the intemperate ought not to be met. Unfortunately the socialist formula is not qualified to take account of this point. This embarrassment is more serious when one appreciates the difficulty of appropriately amending the socialist formula. A standard is required to determine what needs ought to be fulfilled. If needs are simply desires, no standard seems possible; it is doubtful that we can meaningfully speak of some desires being better than others. Moreover, the criticisms raised above demonstrate that an objective account of nonbasic needs suffers difficulties in many cases. Hence, the facts about nonbasic needs required for intelligent moral judgments can be difficult to obtain. It is difficult to know how one could decide what needs ought to be fulfilled.

The socialist might try to avoid this difficulty by arguing that the whole issue rests on a confusion. The problem is not with the needs but with the means of fulfilling them. Smith's need is as legitimate as Jones's. However, Smith has used his share of the poison in an immoral manner. But the socialist formula cannot be criticized simply because Smith used his just share immorally.

Such a reply will not do, however. The moral problem has been pushed one step ahead, but it has not been resolved. Instead of asking what needs ought to be fulfilled, we now ask what means should be used to fulfill needs. The latter question must be answered if we are to be sure how specific commodities are to be distributed. A farmer is entitled to a share of the poison only if we know how he is going to use it. The socialist, however, faces the same difficulties in answering the second question as he does the first. The same theoretical problems remain whether the concern be with needs or with the means to need fulfillment. Moreover, if the socialist formula is to be comprehensive, the second question requires an answer as much as the first. The problem cannot be avoided.

Nonmoral need conflicts. Even if the socialist could resolve all the difficulties above, his problems would not disappear. Many need conflicts are not moral in nature and their occurrence creates difficulties for the socialist formula. First, two men may be in competition for the satisfaction of the same need. Consider the following adaptation of a problem made famous by Braithwaite.[13] Matthew and Luke are neighbors in adjoining nonsoundproof apartments. Both have a need for relaxation, but each fulfills his need in a different way. Matthew plays jazz on the trumpet. Luke, more sedate by nature, plays classical music on the piano. Since they both work long and similar hours, their times for recreation are similar and overlap. Hence they are in conflict. How should the time for recreation be distributed? At this point, something more helpful is required than to suggest that the time be distributed according to need.

Secondly, a similar problem results when the situation above is varied slightly. Matthew and Luke are still neighbors; Matthew still plays jazz and Luke still plays classical music on the piano. However, in this case, Luke plays the piano to satisfy an aesthetic need. At this point, Luke's aesthetic need is in conflict with Matthew's need for relaxation. Only if one need is more urgent than the other, can the socialist formula be of any help here. Actually, the problem is more complex than it first appears. Even if it can be established that Matthew's need for relaxation is more urgent than Luke's aesthetic need, it would certainly be unjust to deprive Luke completely. Certainly some proportion of the time should be allowed to Luke. It seems doubtful that the concept of urgency can be stretched to meet this point. Can we say that two hours for Matthew is more urgent than one hour for Luke, but that two and one-half hours for Matthew is not more urgent than one-half hour for Luke?

Thirdly, conflicts can result between the needs of an individual and the needs of the community. The social security tax discussed in Chapter III provides a good example. Certainly some people have needs which are more urgent than retirement payments. However, they must still contribute to these payments; the system would collapse if they did not. Hence, the urgent needs of some are sacrificed for the urgent needs of the community as a whole. Which needs are really more urgent, and is it possible to say in every case? Most forms of taxation provide similar examples.

13. Richard Braithwaite, *Theory of Games as a Tool for the Moral Philosopher* (Cambridge: Cambridge University Press, 1955), pp. 8–9.

In each of the three cases above, the conflict does not arise from any immoral behavior on the part of the recipients. It results simply from the fact that not all needs can be satisfied simultaneously. However, the socialist formula has no adequate basis for resolving such conflicts; it must remain mute. The criterion of need is not sufficiently comprehensive and other criteria are required to resolve such conflicts.

4. The Practicability of the Socialist Formula

The traditional problem. The best-known and accepted criticism of the socialist formula is its alleged impracticality. The controversy centers on the issue of incentives. It is argued that under the socialist formula there can be a wide gulf between the amount of work done and the remuneration received. Often the neediest are those who produce the least. Hence under the socialist formula an important motive for the hard work of the producers is a concern for the welfare of the less fortunate. Given these facts, the critic argues as follows:

1. Men will not work according to their ability simply to provide for the needs of others.
2. In many cases, however, the socialist formula depends on this altruistic motive as the basis of production.
3. Hence, the socialist formula will not work in practice.

The validity of this argument is the source of intense dispute. Because of the complex economic and factual issues involved, this dispute is beyond my range of competence. The interested reader is referred to some relevant books and articles.[14] My own opinion is that the importance of the argument is more ap-

14. A fine economic discussion of incentive is provided by George F. Break, "The Effects of Taxation on Work Incentives" *Private Wants and Public Needs,* ed. Edmund S. Phelps, rev. ed. (New York: W. W. Norton & Company, Inc., 1965), pp. 55–65. One of the earlier empirical studies is Paul H. Douglas, *The Theory of Wages* (New York: Macmillan Company, 1934). More recent empirical studies include George F. Break, "Income Taxes, Wage Rates, and Incentive to Supply Labor Services" *National Tax Journal,* VI (December, 1953), 350–1, Thomas H. Sanders, *Effects of Taxation on Executives* (Boston: Harvard University, 1951), and Robert Davidson, "Income Taxes and Incentive: The Doctor's Viewpoint," *National Tax Journal* VI (September, 1953), 297; detailed information on the effect of the welfare state in Britain can be found in *Royal Commission on the Taxation of Profits and Income* (2nd report: CMD 9105; London, 1954) and Allan M. Cartter, *The Redistribution of Income in Post-War Britain—A Study of the Effects of the Central Government Fiscal Program in 1948-9,* (New Haven: Yale University Press, 1955), esp. pp. 91–2. For an early socialist discussion, see Annie Besant, "Industry Under Socialism" in *Fabian*

parent than real. In one respect the criticism is irrelevant. The socialist formula is a moral formula and hence is concerned only with what men ought to do, not with what they in fact do. In a realm of moral beings the formula certainly is practical. However, the critic may rightly point out that we do not live in a world of moral beings and an adequate theory for this world must take that into account. The worldliness of the critic need not cause the socialist any great concern, however, for he can point out that in the real world the producer is working for his own needs, not solely for the needs of others. The practical problem decreases as the correspondence between production and reward increases and a wide gap between production and reward is less likely. For these reasons, the traditional objections to the socialist formula seem overrated.

My concern is with practicable problems of a different nature. I am not concerned with determining if men *would* act according to the formula but if they *could* act according to the formula. Is the formula sufficiently specific and comprehensive to be practicably applied?

Practicability of "to each according to his need." The practicable difficulties which concern us here arise directly from the conceptual difficulties discussed in Section 3. The socialist's attempt to specify the basic concepts of the formula make the formula inapplicable to actual distributions in certain cases.

The first problem facing the socialist is the determination of what people really need. If the individual decides what he needs, it is clearly to his advantage to inflate them so he can receive a larger share. In such situations the actual distributions would depend more on the ability to convince those in authority of need than on actual need. The best liars would receive the larger share. Moreover, this kind of social situation is highly unstable. The disputes about genuine needs would be hopeless. Everyone would try to convince those in authority that his need assessments are genuine but that those of his neighbors are highly inflated. Those who must make the actual distributions would be in an unenviable position. Their decisions would not rest on standards of need, but on their convictions as to the sincerity of the recipients.

If, however, the socialist should escape this morass by setting standards of genuine need, questions of liberty are raised. This important problem will be discussed in Section 5.

Secondly, there are always certain scarcity situations in which the socialist formula cannot apply. It must be emphasized that these scarcity problems occur even in extremely productive economic systems. The only society in which they could not occur are societies in which all needs could be satisfied. However, in such societies, there is no longer a problem of distributive justice. The

Essays in Socialism, ed. George Bernard Shaw (New York: Humboldt Publishing Company, 1891), pp. 206–12.

problems of scarcity discussed here are not problems of scarcity in economic systems, but are limited problems of scarcity within categories of various needs. No matter how complex we make our system of need priorities, the supply must be such that only some of the needs within the priority category can be satisfied. An exact matching between supply and priority class would be a rare event. The only way this problem could be completely avoided is by rating the priority of each individual. For each need, every person would be ranked in accordance with his urgency for this need. However, this is clearly impossible. The formidable objections against a general system of need priorities are undoubtedly overwhelming when it must be carried to this point. The problem is a simple one. The socialist formula cannot be made so specific that all scarcity problems can be avoided. When the priorities of need are not sufficiently detailed, a formula of distributive justice based only on need will be inadequate in scarcity situations. These situations have been spelled out in detail in Section 3.

Also in Section 3 we have shown that there are various conflicts which can arise between needs. In each case, however, the socialist formula cannot provide a resolution of the conflicts. The socialist formula cannot apply and hence is not practicable. Significantly, such cases have some scope. These conflicts arise in all tax cases where individual needs are sacrificed for the good of the community. Limitations of time and space also create need conflicts. In crowded industrial areas, such conflicts are the rule rather than the exception. It is not simply a question of Matthew's trumpet vs. Luke's piano. Crowded highways, apartment buildings, and recreation facilities provide a wide range of need conflicts. A formula which can do little to resolve such conflicts is surely impracticable.

The problems of practicability above emerge directly from the conceptual difficulties of the socialist formula. The socialist must specify what he means by "need." However, need is a concept which cannot be plausibly specified in great detail. But failure to specify it completely presents problems of application as has been indicated above. This two-fold difficulty is a socialist's dilemma.

5. Counterexamples

In the final section, two purposes will be accomplished. First, various counterexamples will be presented. These are based on nonsocialist values which should predominate in certain situations. Secondly, I will show that many of the difficulties of Sections 3 and 4 result from the exclusiveness of the socialist formula, i.e., from the omission of competing values. It will be argued that these difficulties could be reduced if these other values had been taken into account. This discussion will provide an excellent introduction to Chapter V. It will illustrate again my contention that the problem of distributive justice is to order conflicting values. To achieve distributive justice, we cannot rely on a formula which emphasizes only some of the competing values.

The socialist's consideration of values. In Section 2, it was shown that the socialist formula bases production on the value of ability and distribution on the value of happiness or well-being. From this initial position, it can be argued that the socialist takes account of other relevant values as well. The socialist formula is compatible with egalitarian formulas of equal treatment. Everyone who has the same need has an equal right to the satisfaction of that need. The socialist adopts the formal egalitarian position that equals should be treated equally and provides content to that formal principle by specifying that those with equal needs should be treated equally. Moreover, if the needs are exactly the same, the distributed commodities should be the same.

The socialist can also argue that his formula takes adequate account of efficiency. On the production side, each man chooses the occupation for which he is most fitted and performs within that occupation according to certain standards. On the distribution side, efficiency occurs because the most urgent needs are met first. "From ability to the most urgent need" is the epitome of an efficient distributive system.

Difficulties with the socialist values. The critic of socialism would quickly dispute the contention that socialism promotes efficiency. This dispute rests on the traditional criticism of the socialist theory of motivation for production. As you recall, this argument stresses that the gap between what a worker produces and what he receives stifles initiative and leads to distortions in the optimum conditions of production. The end result is less for everyone. It must be noted, however, that the truth of this objection depends on the truth of the account of motivation which it presupposes. So long as the truth of the account of motivation is in doubt, the truth of the objection is in doubt. The traditional argument is not as decisive as one would expect. If each worker will produce at capacity, he is certainly producing efficiently in the ordinary meaning of that term.

A more effective argument results when we emphasize ability rather than efficiency. The critic of the socialist's position argues that ability should be as important in distribution as in production. Consider the following proposed distributions in a two-man economy:

	I		II	
	%	%	%	%
	Produced	Received	Produced	Received
A	95	50	95	60
B	05	50	05	40

Assume that A and B have equal needs and that in both proposed distributions A's and B's basic needs are fulfilled. Assume also that B has no physical incapacity. Which of the proposed distributions is the just one? The socialist is committed to I. The distribution is equal because the needs are equal. However, our intuitions would favor II. II seems more just because not only are needs considered, but the productive contribution of the recipient seems relevant as well. If A contributes nearly twenty times as much as B, almost everyone would feel that A should receive more than B, even if A and B provide equal effort. Everyone would be much worse off without the exceptional skill of A. In such situations it seems just that such exceptional ability should be somewhat rewarded. However, the socialist formula makes no provision whatsoever for such reward.

Socialism and liberty. Traditionally, one of the most common criticisms of socialism has been that socialism would require a sacrifice of individual freedom. Usually, this argument has been directed against the increased power of central government which many socialists advocate. However, not all socialists have advocated larger powers for the state. Advocates of highly decentralized government and even anarchists are found in the socialist tradition. In any case, my purpose is not to enter the controversy which swirls about the issue of government power and individual liberty. Instead I seek to demonstrate that a socialist program based on the concepts of ability and need developed thus far presents dangers for the value of liberty.

According to the socialist formula, each person should work according to his ability. At one level, "working according to his ability" means working in the occupation for which he is most fitted. Suppose, however, that someone has the $ability_1$ to be a doctor, but prefers to be a teacher. A socialist would insist that he ought to be a doctor. A libertarian, however, would take a different view. He would insist that the value of liberty has priority when one chooses his occupation. Free choice of occupation is a fundamental right, more important than either ability or efficiency. Hence, contrary to the socialist's view, the man ought not to be a doctor, but ought to be a teacher.

This danger to freedom of occupation is mitigated somewhat when men have $ability_1$ for several occupations, since presumably the socialist would allow them to choose from among the set of occupations for which they have ability$_1$. However, they are still constrained by their ability$_1$ and those with limited ability$_1$ are severely constrained. There is no automatic correspondence between the occupations which men are able$_1$ to undertake and those which they choose to undertake. Strict reliance on ability would require a sacrifice of freedom in certain cases.

Also the socialist method of distribution presents other serious threats to liberty. In Section 3 I have argued that the socialist must give "need" an objective characterization so that needs can be ranked objectively according to urgency. Only in this way can the socialist formula avoid uselessness and be of any assistance as a principle of distribution. In Section 4, I argued that if the socialist formula is to be practicable, distribution cannot be made on the basis of the recipients' claims on need, but instead, must be based on an independent rating of principles. If the independent rating is not used, it is to everyone's advantage to overstate his need so that he will receive more. Hence, it seems that to distribute according to need, the socialist establishes a priority classification of needs on the basis of urgency. Then the socialist determines what commodities will satisfy each need and how much of each commodity various groups of people require. For example, the socialist establishes that food is more important than shelter, shelter than vacations, etc. He then determines how many calories of food, children, women, physical laborers, etc., require.

This independent priority classification is a serious threat to freedom. Only if the list of priorities is accepted unanimously could conflicts with liberty be avoided. However, it seems certain that many people will feel that their individual needs are not accurately reflected in the standards, although there will be little that they can do about it. For if one person can alter the standard in his favor, everyone will try this approach, and the chaos which the standards are designed to avoid will ensue.

Moreover, many individuals will have need priorities which differ from the standard priorities. For example, some people might prefer a longer vacation to adequate housing. Such unique preferences could not be met however, since they would upset the rationing system which the list of priorities is designed to provide. The socialist might attempt to escape this problem by distributing money income only. Then individuals could purchase commodities according to their own priorities and consumer sovereignty would be saved. Such a response will not do, however. How will the socialist determine how much money income each individual is to receive? On socialist principles, the amount must be based on need. But obviously this reintroduces the questions above. Need priorities must be set so that the limited money income can be distributed justly. However, it is precisely this establishing of need priorities which endangers individual freedom.

The dilemma is inescapable. The more the socialist seeks to provide an objective account of needs in specific cases, the more individual freedom he sacrifices. He escapes one horn of the dilemma only to be impaled on the other.

Merit. The socialist formula is also inadequate because it fails to take account of merit in distribution. Suppose that Jones is frequently ill and requires a great deal of medical attention. In each case, the maladies are attributable to Jones's intemperance. He eats heavily and refuses to stay on his prescribed diet. He refuses to exercise and will give up neither smoking nor drinking. As a result he suffers from heart trouble and a variety of intestinal and circulatory disorders. He is unable to work, but his needs are very great.

In this case, should distribution be according to need? Even though Jones's medical needs are properly described as basic, is it just to provide for Jones by depriving others of satisfaction of their nonbasic needs? Jones's needs are his own fault; his illness is his responsibility. At some point it seems unjust to deprive others in order to satisfy the needs of Jones. Similar injustices occur when needs result from excessive gambling, alcoholism, and poor budgetary habits in general. If one refuses treatment or education, it would seem unjust to the other members of society to satisfy the needs of these people. They, not society, are responsible for their needs.

Finally, the socialist formula ignores the fact that some jobs have characteristics which demand extra compensation. Some jobs are characterized by excessive unpleasantness or danger. Even if a man does have an ability$_1$ for defusing bombs, skydiving, or painting skyscrapers, he should receive extra compensation because his job is more than normally dangerous. With such workers, more than need should be considered.

In other jobs, some men expend more effort than others. John Ryan uses the example of the ditch digger and the driver of the dump wagon to illustrate his point.[15] Since the ditch digger exerts so much more effort, justice demands that the ditch digger receive more. It is effort, not need, that counts in this case.

The above difficulties arise because what men contribute is not theoretically linked to what they receive. Where the natural overlapping between the two breaks down, counterexamples are generated. When the conditions of production are divorced from distribution, the socialist formula errs in several ways by not considering the merit of the recipient.

Relation of Sections 3, 4, and 5. The above counterexamples result from the exclusiveness of the socialist formula. In certain situations needs are not the sole, or even the most important, consideration for just distributions. Liberty, ability, and merit are always important and sometimes decisive.

15. John Ryan, *Distributive Justice* (New York: Macmillan Company, 1942), p. 182.

Moreover, the exclusiveness of the socialist formula lies at the foundation of the other difficulties. Suppose that distributions could be made on the basis of other values beside need. If this were the case, the scarcity problems and need conflicts of Sections 3 and 4 could be resolved by an appeal to other values. The dilemma presented by the socialist's attempt to specify "need" could be avoided. Need priorities would be established only when the needs are objective or are agreed upon by all. As the establishment of need priority becomes more and more difficult, distributions will be based on other values. However, to move in this direction would be to abandon the socialist formula.

6. Conclusion

The analysis above should demonstrate that the socialist formula cannot serve as an adequate formula of distributive justice. It suffers the same inadequacy and hence the same fate as utilitarianism and egalitarianism. It is too restricted, i.e., it fails to consider and accommodate all the values necessary if just distributions are to be made in all cases. Perhaps what is needed is not a more sophisticated formula but a different approach. It is this different approach which will be the concern of Chapter V.

V. Towards a New Theory of Distributive Justice

IN THE past three chapters I have demonstrated the inadequacy of the three traditional formulas of distributive justice. Significantly, these inadequacies result even when the formulas are interpreted most favorably. More significantly, they have common failures. Why do the traditional formulas fail? First, they fail because their adherents do not understand the nature of the problem of distributive justice. The problem is not to select one principle and apply it in all cases. Instead, the problem is to choose among legitimate values and principles and to order them as the situation warrants. Secondly, the traditional formulas are not sufficiently inclusive. In Chapter I, I isolated six values which should be considered before a decision concerning distributive justice is made. However, the traditional formulas do not take all of these relevant values into consideration. This inadequacy makes them vulnerable to counterexamples. Thirdly, the adherents to the traditional formulas demand too much of them. The formulas cannot be applied in every situation. Such universal applicability would require that the terms of the formula be applicable to highly specific and precise situations. However, I have shown that the terms of the traditional formulas are not applicable in this way.

From these failures, two important lessons can be learned. First, an increased awareness of the complexity of the problem of distributive justice rules out the one-formula approach. Secondly, the complexities of the problem in conjunction with the lack of complete applicability to precise situations make the search for universal principles unrealistic. A more humble, but more accurate perspective views formulas of distributive justice as guides.

Those who have become skeptical of the traditional formulas have often appealed to one of three alternatives. First, the search for principles of just distribution is abandoned. Instead some natural distribution such as that achieved by the might of the stronger, majority opinion, or the natural working of the economic system is accepted. However, the adoption of this course eliminates a concern for justification and hence there is no longer an attempt to achieve distributive *justice*. Obviously this approach is not adequate for my purposes. The second approach is to limit principles of distributive justice to formal principles. The Aristotelian formula is one example of this approach.[1] However, this restricted approach is not adequate for my purposes since the important material principles are not provided. More than formal principles are required for a comprehensive theory. The third alternative is to judge each distributive situation on its own merits. For this approach there are no principles of distributive justice; there are only particular moral decisions about what is just or unjust in specific situations. Once principles are given up, however, on what basis can the just distribution be determined? Such an alternative seems committed to some sort of intuitionism for every case. Our intuitions may agree in clear-cut cases and hence be acceptable. However, they certainly do not agree in every case. For this reason, our intuitions are unacceptable and need to be supplemented by principles for resolving the harder cases. The third alternative is also inadequate.

The alternative proposed by this writer is to chart a middle course between two extremes. On the one hand, I must avoid formulas which allegedly apply in all situations. On the other hand, I must avoid alternatives which propose that the search for principles of distributive justice be given up. What is required are some general flexible principles and some indication of the situations to which they apply. The purpose of this chapter is to make a start in this direction. To accomplish this goal the chapter is divided into six sections. In Section 1, various rival formal criteria of distributive justice are discussed and my own proposed criterion is adopted. In Section 2, I discuss the role of a model as an aid in philosophical investigation. Various models for distributive justice are considered and an aspect of the language model is proposed for adoption. Section 3 is a section of classification and characterization. Most of the attention is given to a characterization of the six values and a classification of the various types of societies. In Sections 4 and 5, I utilize the language model to provide the principles of distributive justice. In Section 6, I provide an evaluation of the results.

1. A Formal Criterion of Distributive Justice

The purpose of this section is to provide an adequate formal criterion of distributive justice. A formal criterion provides a necessary condition for all just distributions. A brief discussion of the Aristotelian criterion and a lengthy discussion of the theory of John Rawls precede my own proposed criterion.

1. Aristotle, *Nicomachean Ethics,* Book V, trans. Martin Ostwald (New York: Bobbs-Merrill Company, Inc., 1962).

Aristotle. Aristotle's discussion in book five of *Nicomachean Ethics* seems rather complicated, although in fact it is fairly simple.[2] Aristotle maintains that the just is equal, but that it is an equality of the ratios of the persons and the shares. If A and B are equal in some relevant respect M, then their shares should be equal. If they are unequal with respect to M, their shares should be in proportion to M and hence the ratio of their shares to their possession of M is equal:

$$\frac{\text{Share for A}}{\text{A's Possession of M}} = \frac{\text{Share for B}}{\text{B's Possession of M}}$$

The principal is formal because, as Aristotle points out, one can choose any criterion for desert one wishes. The principle is compatible with any criterion. The principle only insists that once the criterion has been established, the ratios should be equal. A similar egalitarian criterion was proposed as E_3 in Chapter III.[3] The same difficulties apply here. If the criterion is meant to refer to the equal distribution of commodities, then it fails in extreme scarcity situations, like the ice-floe example. When the supply of commodities is insufficient to maintain the lives of the recipients, it is not a necessary condition of distributive justice to give equals to equals. If, on the other hand, the criterion is meant to refer to equal treatment, we face the conceptual and practicable difficulty of deciding how equal treatment is possible. The "one man–one" vote form of equal treatment can result in majority injustice to the minority. Unanimity, however, is impracticable because it allows one individual to thwart the goals of the community solely for individual gain. Intermediate positions fail on one or both of the above grounds. Neither equal distribution for equals nor equal treatment is free from difficulty.

Secondly, Aristotle makes equality a formal value. He does not give it a material and substantive role in distributive justice. A distribution is not made because it provides for equality. The only function of the equality principle is to set a condition on distributions made on the basis of other values. Equality has a more substantive role in distributive justice than that of being a constraining condition. When specified in terms of rights, equality determines the just distribution. It is my contention that none of the six values functions merely formally. For this reason it could be misleading to build any of them into the formal criterion. The formal criterion should provide a necessary condition for distributive justice without making any of the individual values necessary conditions of distributive justice.

John Rawls. A different type of formal theory is that presented by John Rawls. Rawls focuses his attention on the *procedure* of distributive justice. His con-

2. *Ibid.*, pp. 118–20.
3. See Chapter III p. 52 ff.

cern is not with the justice of individual distributions, but with the overall procedure.

Now an essential feature of this whole scheme is that it contains an element of pure procedural justice. That is, no attempt is made to specify the just distribution of particular goods and services to particular persons, as if there were only one way in which, independently of the choices of economic agents, these things should be shared. Rather, the idea is to design a scheme such that the resulting distribution, whatever it is, which is brought about by the efforts of those engaged in cooperation and elicited by their expectations, is just. . . . Given a just constitution and the smooth working of the four branches of government, and so on, there exists a procedure such that the actual distribution of wealth, whatever it turns out to be, is just.[4]

This procedure is embodied in just social institutions. The plan for these just institutions is a social contract which has been accepted by all in a condition of equal liberty. In addition Rawls has two principles of justice which play the central role in all of Rawls's published work on justice.

1. Each person engaged in an institution or affected by it has an equal right to the most extensive liberty compatible with a like liberty for all.
2. Inequalities as defined by the institutional structure or fostered by it are arbitrary unless it is reasonable to expect that they will work out to everyone's advantage and provided the positions and offices to which they attach or from which they may be gained are open to all.[5]

It appears that Rawls means these conditions to apply both to the making of the social contract and to the content of the contract made.[6] With respect to the actual contract of the institutions for distributive justice, Rawls provides a specific interpretation of principle (2). This interpretation is designed to rule out a utilitarian interpretation of the institutions for distributive justice. Rawls insists that the inequalities must work out to the advantage of the least fortunate.

We interpret the second principle to hold that these differences are just

4. John Rawls, "Distributive Justice" in *Philosophy, Politics, and Society,* ed. Peter Laslett and W. G. Runciman, 3rd series (New York: Barnes & Noble, Inc., 1967), pp. 76-8.
5. *Ibid.,* p. 61. These two principles are central to every article published by Rawls on justice.
6. In John Rawls, "Justice as Fairness," *Philosophical Review* LXVII (1958), the principles seem to apply to the making of the contract, especially principle one. See esp. pp. 165ff. In "Distributive Justice" they clearly apply to the economic institutions as well. See esp. pp. 61-2.

if and only if the greater expectations of the more advantaged, when play-ing a part in the working of the whole social system, improve the expecta-tions of the least advantaged. The basic structure is just throughout when the advantages of the more fortunate promote the well-being of the least fortunate, that is when a decrease in their advantages would make the least fortunate even worse off than they are. The basic structure is per-fectly just when the prospects of the least fortunate are as great as they can be.[7]

Rawls then goes on to sketch a theory which has some resemblance to that of economic utilitarianism discussed in Chapter II. This account of distributive justice merits serious attention. It is complex, influential, and has several ob-vious advantages. A procedural approach would greatly simplify the problem if it would work. To be able to eliminate concern with individual distributions and concentrate on the procedures for justice is highly economical. Moreover, once the just procedures are determined, for the most part, the problem of distributive justice would be solved; we would be confident that all resulting distributions are just. The most that would be required is a policing action to make sure the procedures are not violated. Finally, Rawls seems to understand the complicated nature of problems of distributive justice. His simple approach does not rest on faulty analysis. He correctly views the problem of justice as one of adjusting competing claims.

Justice is the virtue of practices where there are assumed to be competing interests and conflicting claims, and where it is supposed that persons will press their rights on each other. . . . justice requires the elimination of arbitrary distinctions and the establishment within its (institutional) struc-ture of a proper balance of equilibrium between competing claims. Princi-ples of justice specify when the balance or share is proper and which distinctions are arbitrary. . . .[8]

Objections. In spite of the advantages, Rawls' conception of formal procedural justice is inadequate. The first major difficulty is to determine a process for establishing the social contract. The difficulty of interpreting Rawls's first prin-ciple in terms of "one man–one vote" has been discussed in Chapter III. Since the contract is made by rational egoists, it is certainly possible that the majority treat the minority unjustly. On the other hand, if Rawls wants unanimity, one

7. Rawls, "Distributive Justice," p. 66.
8. Rawls, "Justice as Fairness," p. 175, and John Rawls, "Constitutional Liberty and the Concept of Justice" in Nomos VI Justice, ed. Carl Friedrich and John Chapman (New York: Atherton Press, 1962), p. 99. The point that distributive justice is best understood in terms of competing claims is an important conclusion of Professor Rescher's Distributive Justice.

man could hold out for an unfair advantage. To avoid such criticisms, Rawls has ingeniously adopted a procedure which rules them out. Those who establish the contract do not know what position they will have in the resulting society. Hence the most rational procedure is to act as if one's enemy were going to assign the positions. If everyone adopts this assumption, the social contract will be designed so that the least advantaged will be as well off as possible and Rawls's second principle can be fulfilled. Actually, Rawls needs another assumption if his principle of ignorance is to work. He must assume that none of the contractees will gamble, i.e., that no one desires to establish positions of privilege and then take his chances on obtaining them.
In developing the principle of ignorance, however, Rawls runs afoul of another difficulty. The social contract

> . . . assumes that the individuals who belong to society must choose together, in one joint act, what is to count among them as just and unjust. They are to decide among themselves *once and for all* what is to be their conception of justice.[9]

However, it is practicably impossible to make a social contract once and for all in one joint act. Braybrooke and Lindblom have presented a devastating critique of this form of social engineering in their book, *A Strategy of Decision*. Seven of their objections can be applied directly to Rawls's methodology. One cannot decide in one joint act once and for all what is just and unjust because:

1. In deciding matters of justice one does not choose between clear-cut alternatives. It is a question of sacrificing a portion of some value in order to gain a portion of another.
2. Problems are continuous; they cannot be settled once and for all. The alleviation of one difficulty will create another.
3. The set of relevant variables is not closed as it would need to be if a decision were made once and for all.
4. No account is taken of changing needs.
5. Such comprehensiveness in planning exceeds man's limited problem-solving capacities.
6. The necessary information is not available.
7. In some cases, the costliness of information exceeds its value.

Braybrooke and Lindblom marshall a great deal of empirical evidence to support their contentions above.[10]
Rawls faces the kind of difficulties a utilitarian faces when he must consider

---

9. Rawls, "Distributive Justice," p. 59. Emphasis mine.
10. David Braybrooke and Charles Lindblom, *A Strategy of Decision* (New York: Free Press, 1963). See esp. Part One and footnotes.

all the consequences of his actions. No social contract can be sufficiently comprehensive to cover all possible situations. One does not design a just social
system the way one designs a house.

The social contract form of procedural justice is vulnerable on moral grounds
as well. John Chapman's criticism is that Rawls's concept of justice has swal-
lowed up the concept of rights. He insists that Rawls does not allow for rights
which would put a limit on agreements. For example, slavery would be just if
it were consented to in the contract.[11] The force of Chapman's remarks is to
raise philosophical questions concerning the obligatoriness of contracts. Does
a man have a right to enter into any contract he desires? Is his freedom unlimited in this respect? If his freedom is unlimited, as Rawls seems to indicate, a
man can enter a contract to have another take his life or a woman would be
entitled to be a prostitute. Many would find such contracts morally abhorrent
because at least one of the parties would be surrendering his self-respect or
dignity.

The moral problem becomes even more serious when we remember that the
contract is made once and for all. Why should future generations be morally
bound by a constitution determined by their forefathers? Certainly this is
unjust. Freedom of contract should not be the privilege of one generation.
Rawls's attempt to provide justice in establishing the contract has put him in
a dilemma. On the one hand, he must escape the difficulties inherent in providing a voting procedure for establishing the contract. He can do this only by
combining a principle of ignorance with a unanimous voting procedure. Moreover, the contract must be made once and for all because in the future the
signers will obviously know their places. On the other hand, to require the
contract to be made once and for all is both unjust and impracticable.

The final difficulty I wish to consider concerns Rawls's two principles of procedural justice. As you recall, Rawls's principles are:

1. Each person engaged in an institution or affected by it has an equal
   right to the most extensive liberty compatible with a like liberty for all.
2. Inequalities, as defined by the institutional structure or fostered by it
   are arbitrary unless it is reasonable to expect that they will work out
   to everyone's advantage and provided the positions and offices to
   which they attach or from which they may be gained are open to all.

I contend that Rawls's two principles can give inconsistent results. Ironically,
Rawls does not realize that his own theory is vulnerable to the same objections he raises against others. He criticizes the nonprocedural approach as
follows:

11. John Chapman, "Justice and Fairness" in *Nomos VI Justice,* pp. 166-7.

For every arrangement combining a particular total welfare with a particular degree of inequality one has simply to decide, without the guidance from principle, how much of an increase (or decrease) in total welfare, say, compensates for a given decrease (or increase) in equality.[12]

Yet the potential for conflict and the problem of balancing competing claims is clearly found in Rawls's two principles. Principle (1) focuses on liberty and principle (2) focuses on the equal right of the least advantaged to the highest living standard possible. If we interpret principle (1) as the right to dispose of one's income as he pleases, then certainly principles (1) and (2) can come into conflict. Implicitly, Rawls seems to recognize that some accommodation seems required when he says of principle (2) that the long-term expectations of the least advantaged are raised to the *highest level consistent with the demands of equal liberty*.[13] But this attempt to balance equality and liberty creates the same kind of difficulties Rawls has raised against others. However, what Rawls might say is that the resulting loss of freedom in society to dispose of one's income in order to provide for the disadvantaged is consistent with the original condition of liberty in which the contracting parties freely gave up some of this freedom over income. In making the contract, some loss of freedom over income was accepted in order to raise the least advantaged to the highest level possible. Then, however, the second principle does not need to be qualified so that it is consistent with the demands of equal liberty. Principle (2) is already consistent with equal liberty because the principle, on this interpretation, results from a contract made by equals. Rawls's reference to consistency only confuses the issue.

However, if we solve the problem in this way, it must be pointed out that Rawls's two principles are no longer on the same logical level. The right to liberty is a formal principle for making contracts, and the principle of an equal right to the highest possible living standard for the disadvantaged is a formal principle for the kind of contract allowed. Rawls cannot have it both ways. If the two principles are applied at once they conflict. Freedom over income is diminished so that equality can be provided. If, on the other hand, the principles are applied at different levels so that some loss of freedom of income had already been accepted, Rawls should make this clear to his readers and clarify his reference to consistency in principle (2). Until this is done the relation between Rawls's two principles is "fuzzy" at best. In general, however, Rawls's theory of pure procedural justice is inadequate on theoretical and practicable grounds.

12. Rawls, "Distributive Justice," p. 80.
13. *Ibid.*, p. 72.

A new formal principle of distributive justice. My own view is that a formal principle should give an indication of the conceptual nature of the problem, but that it should not by itself settle any of the substantive issues. The following principle is adopted for this purpose:

> FP: A distribution is just if and only if it results from a correct application and ordering of the relevant values.

The principle is meant to be a necessary and sufficient condition for any just distribution. It reflects the conceptual nature of the problem without making any particular value a necessary condition of distributive justice. As a formal principle it is an empty principle; it does not tell us what values apply and how they should be ordered. This, however, is as it should be if none of the substantive questions are to be begged. Material principles of distributive justice will be provided in the following sections.

2. Models of Distributive Justice

The formal principle of distributive justice must be enriched by material principles which supply the necessary content. In order to accomplish this difficult task, it seems desirable to consider various types of models which might illustrate the nature of the required material principles. Hence, a brief description of a model and its use in philosophical inquiry seems in order.

The use of models is such a common procedure that we are often unaware of it. We are all familiar with the Hollywood stage set of Dodge City, the architect's blueprint, and the ordinary roadmap. These are models for the western city, the skyscraper, and the highway respectively. Philosophers use models as well. Plato used the model of the state to provide an understanding of man. Galileo, Newton, and Descartes developed the geometrical and mechanical models which provide a very different understanding of man.

In each case, the clear and well-known is used to illuminate the obscure and unknown. One purpose of a model is to use our understanding of one thing to enable us to understand a different thing. For example, in chemistry the solar system is the model which provides an understanding of the structure of the atom. This technique is very similar to the use of a metaphor.[14] In fact, a model has been defined as a sustained metaphor. A model, then, is a heuristic device which aids and clarifies thinking in a dark and murky area.

14. Colin Turbayne, *The Myth of Metaphor* (New Haven: Yale University Press, 1962), p. 19.

This heuristic feature of the model should be emphasized. I use a model to make my analysis of distributive justice clearer and more persuasive. However, the adequacy of my claims about distributive justice is independent of the model I use to explicate them. If a reader does not find the model helpful, he may wish to discard it and consider my claims on distributive justice in their own right.

It must also be emphasized that in utilizing a model it is not necessary that all the features of the object which provides the model apply to the object to be modelled. We select those features and only those features which are useful to us. For example, suppose one suggested a wolf as a model to understand man. The suggestion does not entail that every wolfish characteristic applies to man. The suggestion is only that some wolfish characteristics give us an understanding of the nature of men. We put into our model only those characteristics which are of use to us.

It is important to remember that although a model is an extremely useful device, it is nonetheless a sophisticated form of make-believe; otherwise one is victimized by the model.[15] It is an easy, but fallacious, step to move from (a) Machines help us understand the nature of man, to (b) Man is a machine. Models must be used with caution.

Finally, for any given problem, not all models are equally adequate. The most parsimonious and economical model has a theoretical advantage. Most importantly, models which present false analogies are to be avoided. The most adequate model is the economical one which provides the most adequate analogy. The remainder of this section is devoted to the task of finding a suitable model to aid with the problem of distributive justice.

Math-calculation problems. Perhaps a problem of distributive justice is like a problem of calculation in mathematics. This is certainly the model of utilitarianism. The variables are quantified, the measurements are made, the calculations are performed, and a certain result obtained. This model is a prestigious one. It has been applied with great success in the natural sciences and is now energetically applied in the social sciences.

Nonetheless, it is an inappropriate model for problems of distributive justice. The values which constitute the variables cannot be mathematically quantified. All the problems with the quantitative aspects of the two utilitarianisms discussed in Chapter II are relevant here. A problem of distributive justice is not a problem where precise mathematical terms apply, and more importantly, precise answers are not possible. Since the solutions are not highly precise, a model which requires highly precise solutions is inappropriate.

15. *Ibid.,* pp. 21–7.

Scientific generalizations. For similar reasons a principle of distributive justice cannot be understood as analogous to scientific laws. A scientific law has two features which distinguish it from a principle of distributive justice. First the principles under which a scientific law applies are rather precisely known. Secondly scientific laws are best stated when they are stated in highly quantifiable terms. Neither of these conditions hold for principles of distributive justice.

The criminal-trial procedure. Recently the scientific and mathematical models have been criticized on grounds similar to those above. Such models are inappropriate to ethics in general and to justice in particular. The suggested replacement is to look at problems of justice the way a criminal court judge looks at a defendant.[16] Solving a problem of distributive justice is like reaching a decision in court.

Although the model of the criminal trial marks an improvement, it is still inadequate. Determining a just distribution is not like using flexible procedures to determine whether something is or is not the case. Although there is an analogy between the types of reasoning involved, there is no analogy between the problems which are to be resolved. In the trial the focus is on a particular situation, e.g., Did Sam kill Ted? In distributive justice, we are trying to apply and arrange conflicting values in order to achieve a result. Moreover, in a criminal trial, there is a definite procedure that is adopted to get the result. However, what is missing with the problem of distributive justice is an acceptable procedure. If the trial analogy is meant to suggest that we adopt the procedure in the courts as the procedure for distributive justice, the model is inappropriate. Because the problem is different, a different procedure is needed. If the model is meant to suggest only that it is the procedure, and not the result, which is important, the model again breaks down. The problem of distributive justice is precisely that there is no acceptable procedure for reaching distributive justice as there is for determining criminal justice.

Artistic creativity. A very promising model is artistic creativity. Solving a problem of distributive justice is like creating a symphony. Just as a composer uses a small number of notes to build up musical themes, the social philosopher uses a small number of values to build up just distributions. There are many symphonies, and similarly there are many just distributions. Moreover, just as the composer uses certain principles to combine notes to form the symphony, the social philosopher uses certain principles to combine and order the values to achieve distributive justice.

The theoretical drawback with this model is the role of the principles. The

16. See esp. C. H. Perelman, *Justice* (New York: Random House, Inc., 1967).

artist has principles which he uses to guide the creative process. However, we still search for principles to use for combining and ordering the values. What is needed for our task is a model which illuminates the principles of distributive justice. There is also a practical drawback. The good model uses a well-understood aspect of our experience to enlighten an obscure aspect. Unfortunately, artistic creativity is not especially luminous and is certainly not well understood by this writer. Although something might be done with the artistic creativity model, the disadvantages above make it not quite suitable for my purposes.

The language model.[17] In general what I propose is to use as a model principles for communicating in a language L limited to three-word sentences. Hence, I am utilizing certain principles for communicating in a language to serve as a model for constructing principles of distributive justice. The emphasis on language in twentieth-century philosophy should solve the familiarity problem which plagues the artistic creativity model. Insights into the nature of language are already often used to resolve philosophical problems.

Although the language model is a complicated one, its power to illuminate the construction of different, complicated principles of distributive justice is quite startling. Recall, however, that the model is being used only as a heuristic device. The language model will now be sketched out in some detail.

To communicate in a language L, we need the following rules: We need spelling (formation) rules for combining the letters into words. We also need two types of syntax rules: syntax rules for determining what kinds of words appear in well-formed sentences of the language L, and syntax rules determining the order of the various words. Finally, there are context rules determining what to say in given situations. For example, when giving directions, be clear and precise. Context rules enable us to adapt our language to situations in the world.

To each of these kinds of principles for communicating in a language L, there are analogous principles in the justice language J. There are spelling rules for making justice words out of letters, syntax rules determining what justice words appear in all well-formed justice sentences and in what order, and finally there are context rules which give prescriptions for certain situations.

It may be that the logical status of the rules for communicating in a language

17. The language model was suggested in the later dialogues of Plato, especially *The Sophist, Statesman,* and *Philebus.* Recently Colin Turbayne has argued that Berkeley uses this model in the *Principles.* Turbayne is currently using this model in his own work on metaphysics and has inspired this writer to attempt to apply the model to social ethics. Professor Turbayne has completed an article using this model entitled "Berkeley's Metaphysical Grammar" in Berkeley, *Principles of Human Knowledge,* Text and Critical Essays, Colin Murray Turbayne, ed. (New York: Bobbs-Merrill Company, Inc., 1970) pp. 3–36.

L is not clear. For example, is the statement of a syntax rule an analytical statement, an empirical generalization about how the language L is spoken, an imperative, or what? Obviously this same question can be asked about ethical
rules, as readers in contemporary meta-ethical theory are well aware. Without
trying to settle this issue I propose to construe the rules of both the model
and the thing modelled as hypothetical imperatives:

MODEL	THING MODELLED
If you wish to communicate in the language L, use the following rules . . .	If you wish to construct a just economic system, use the following rules . . .

It should be noted, however, that to construe our rules as hypothetical imperatives is not to make them arbitrary. Imperatives can be supported by reasons, as the work of R. M. Hare and others has shown.

Finally, it should be noted that principles for communicating in a language
can be complicated in two ways. First, the principles may have to be qualified.
For example, the spelling rule "*i* before *e*" has to be qualified, "except after *c*
and in syllables that sound like *a* as in *neighbor* and *weigh*." Secondly, situations may occur which are so complicated that we do not clearly know how to
apply the context rules. There may be situations of such complication that
communication is difficult. Where these complications in our analysis arise,
they will be duly noted. With this general analysis before us, let us consider
the features of the language model in more detail. Before this task is completed, however, some definitions and classifications are required.

3. Definitions and Classifications

The purpose of this section is to provide the necessary information and characterization which is required for the complete formulation of the principles
of distributive justice.

Values. The first task is to characterize satisfactorily the six values adopted in
Chapter I. Values are of such a nature that this characterization cannot be done
with great precision. Theories of distribution, such as utilitarianism and socialism, which require precise characterization of the values seem doomed to

failure. However, if a theory of distributive justice is to be adequate, the characterization must be sufficient to provide a knowledge of what we seek to achieve in distribution and an ability to distinguish one value from the other.

Happiness refers to the psychological feeling of satisfaction. Much happiness is achieved through need satisfaction. It is important that happiness not be confused with other values. The fact that we are free may provide us happiness, but freedom is not a subspecies of happiness, and we do not value freedom because it makes us happy.

Liberty has both a positive and a negative characterization. These characterizations were presented in Chapter III as libertarian positions L_2 and L_1 respectively. The characterizations are repeated below:

Negative freedom: S is free to do x only if S does x without being coerced by some other agent S'.

Positive freedom: S is free to do x at t if and only if
- (1) S has the ability to do x at t and
- (2) There is some alternative y such that
  - (a) S has the ability to do y at t
  - (b) S knows of the opportunity to do y at t
  - (c) y would enable S to achieve his purpose if he wanted to do it
  - (d) no other agent S' coerces S to do x instead of y.

Negative freedom is the value which one usually tries to achieve directly in a just productive system. This is the freedom to choose one's occupation. Positive freedom is often referred to as freedom of opportunity. Positive freedom is the value which one tries to achieve in certain distributive situations. Specific distributions of appropriate resources provide people the ability and knowledge necessary to achieve their goals. This is roughly what is meant by freedom of opportunity. Education is usually considered necessary for freedom of opportunity. Later in this chapter, I shall show how positive freedom is incorporated into principles of distributive justice. I shall also provide a specific example of how positive freedom can enhance negative freedom.

Equality refers to certain rights which all men possess. The right assumed in Chapter III will be assumed here as well.

R_1: Everyone has an equal right to liberty so long as he does not interfere with the liberty of others.

R_2: Everyone has an equal right to a certain standard of living.

It is recognized that these rights must be specified further in particular situations.

Ability refers to those skills possessed by men which enable them to contribute to the well-being of society, including themselves.

Optimization is synonymous with efficiency. Both refer to the method of achieving a given result at least cost.

Merit is the value which is most difficult to define adequately. In a general way merit can be characterized as a quality possessed by either men or products which entitles them to special consideration in production or distribution. In other words, if some product A has the value M and another B does not, this is a good reason to make sure that A has priority in production. What is to count as an M quality will depend on the circumstances.

Although the above characterization of the six values is very general, it does provide us with a common framework. Further specificity will be provided as the discussion proceeds.

A classification of societies.[18] The principles of distributive justice which I shall construct on the language model are principles for a just distributive system. The principles are designed for application to the various economic systems. To construct the appropriate number of principles, an adequate classification of societies according to their productive capabilities is required. The classification is of a general type, and societies do fall between the categories. This fact need cause no difficulty if the state of intermediacy can be recognized and principles of distributive justice applied.

First, a society is in a situation of extreme scarcity whenever the supply of commodities is such that it is impossible to meet all the basic needs of its members. That is, it is impossible to prevent some from dying of starvation, exposure, etc. In this case even the barest minimum standard of living is not possible for all. Fortunately, this situation occurs but rarely.

Secondly, a society is in a subsistence situation whenever its resources can just provide a minimum standard of living for all its members. The concept of a minimum standard of living is a biological and physiological one. Hence, it can be determined with considerable objectivity. A family has a minimum standard of living when it has the resources to stay alive and to remain sufficiently healthy for contribution to the productive effort. Life is certainly not pleasant in such a society but everyone can exist there. The family resources are limited to minimum amounts of food, clothing, shelter, and medical care.

Thirdly, a society may be described as comfortable whenever its productive resources are such that a minimum standard of decency is available for all. The concept of a minimum standard of decency is different in kind from that of a minimum standard of living. Whereas the latter is biological in nature, the former is psychological and political in nature. In trying to specify the concept, one must avoid the dangers which undermined socialism. It is fruitless to attempt

18. This classification recognizes the point of Professor Rescher in his book *Distributive Justice*. Just distributions depend upon the capabilities of economic systems.

an exhaustive definition and ranking of nonbasic needs. An understanding of the concept of a minimum standard of decency cannot be achieved in that way.

The concept is a complicated one which can be best characterized by specifying its three parts. Families have a minimum standard of decency when (a) they have a minimum standard of living, (b) when they have the resources which can provide them with positive liberty (freedom of opportunity), and (c) when the income differential between those families with less income and those with more income is not excessive.

This characterization of a minimum standard of decency has several advantages. First, it is general in the sense that it does not specify the exact constituents of a minimum standard of decency for all cases. This generality is necessary if the concept is to be plausible and the objections against utilitarianism and socialism are to be avoided.

Secondly, however, the concept is determinate in the sense that we can know when a society has achieved a minimum standard of decency, although there are several steps at which this determination is to be made. The determination of condition (a) is scientific. Condition (c) is politically determined by measuring social discontent. As those families who receive the least income find the differential becoming wider and wider, a point will be reached at which they will show their discontent. When this discontent expresses itself in social unrest, riots, strikes, etc., it can be said that the income of these families has fallen below the minimum standard of decency. Condition (c) is violated in such cases. The determination of condition (b) is partly scientific and partly political. On the scientific side, psychologists and other social scientists can say that freedom from ignorance and freedom from the insecurities of accident, old age, and unemployment are necessary conditions for freedom of opportunity. Hence resources should be distributed so that these necessary conditions are met and the value of freedom of opportunity can be achieved. Social scientists may add to this list of necessary conditions at any time. In these respects the determination of condition (b) is scientific and resembles the determination of a minimum standard of living.

Other aspects of condition (b) are not scientific, however. Neither the non-necessary conditions of freedom of opportunity nor the specific resources required to achieve the necessary conditions of freedom of opportunity can be determined scientifically. For example, in the United States, a paid two-week vacation is considered a part of a minimum standard of decency. Some recreation is considered necessary for freedom of opportunity and the two-week vacation is accepted as a norm. It is a standard aspect of one's employment contract. In many parts of the world and earlier in United States history, however, a paid vacation is and was a luxury. The actual resources provided for freedom of opportunity are culturally determined. In other cases, a cultural norm is not available and it is extremely difficult to determine just what an individual's needs and abilities are. In such cases equal distribution is a reasonable way to eliminate that practical problem.

In conclusion, the determination of condition (b), freedom of opportunity, depends on both scientific and nonscientific factors. Hence, although it is true that the constituents of a minimum standard of decency cannot be determined precisely for all societies, guidelines for determining a minimum standard of decency are provided. One can tell whether a society has or has not achieved a minimum standard of decency. This is no mean achievement and is sufficient for our purposes.

Thirdly, the concept of a minimum standard of decency is very broad and can be achieved in stages. This quality of piecemeal achievability is very advantageous, as we shall see, when justice and efficiency are discussed later in the chapter.

The next society to be considered is the affluent society. In the affluent society, the level of production far exceeds the requirements for a minimum standard of living and freedom of opportunity. Food, clothing, housing, education, medical facilities, and recreational facilities are available in great abundance and variety. In addition, there are large numbers of goods and services available for newly discovered consumer wants. All citizens possess some of the new household gadgets, attend places of recreation, enjoy at least an occasional dinner out at a restaurant, and engage themselves productively with increased leisure time.

Finally, I must speak briefly of societies in the intermediate stages. The only intermediate societies of interest for our purposes are those that fall between subsistence and comfort and those that fall between comfort and affluence. Most societies, in fact, fall into one of these two intermediary stages. A society cannot be between extreme scarcity and subsistence. Either you can keep everyone alive or you cannot. This does not deny, of course, that a society can be mistaken, i.e., that it may think it is in a situation of extreme scarcity and not be. On the other extreme, I contend that at this point it is not necessary for purposes of distributive justice to distinguish among affluent societies. Principles of distributive justice are only required for two remaining intermediary stages, that is for those between subsistence and comfort and for those between comfort and affluence.

Special definitions. The following terms will play an important part in the development of my principles of distributive justice. For purposes of convenience they are defined below at this time:

Economic income: Economic income is that income which one receives as payment for his contribution to production. It depends on such economic factors as amount of time worked, marginal productivity, and the supply of labor for that job, as well as the demand for the product.

Merit good: A merit good is a good whose amount of production should not depend solely on the forces operating in a competitive market, i.e., the amount produced does not represent the amount that would be produced if consumer demand as expressed in the market were followed exactly.

Public good: A public good is one whose consumption by one individual does not reduce its utility to any other individual.[19] Such goods have the characteristic of nonappropriability discussed in Chapter II. Since the preferences of these goods as expressed in the market should not be used as a guide to production, public goods are a special class of merit goods.

Minimum standard of living: A person is said to have a minimum standard of living if he has sufficient goods for survival and general health.

4. The Rules of Principle Construction

Having sketched out the nature of a model and having completed our classification of economic systems, we can now utilize the language model to construct principles of distributive justice. We begin this task by developing the justice alphabet.

Features of the model-letters and values. The thesis of this book is that problems of distributive justice are resolved by applying and ordering the relevant values. Just as letters of an alphabet are the basic elements of a sentence, the values of Chapter I are the basic elements of a principle of just distributive systems. The justice alphabet will contain six letters, one letter for each value. The justice alphabet and the corresponding values are provided below:

	VALUES	LETTERS
1.	Happiness	H
2.	Liberty	L
3.	Equality	E
4.	Optimization (Efficiency)	O
5.	Merit	M
6.	Ability (Skill)	A

19. William Baumol, *Welfare Economics and the Theory of the State,* 2nd ed. (Cambridge, Mass.: Harvard University Press, 1965), p. 20.

In any alphabet, some letters are vowels and the remainder are consonants. Vowels are letters which enter into a large number of letter combinations. Vowels facilitate word formation. Plato noted this greater combining power of vowels in the *Sophist*.[20] I designate happiness and liberty as the vowels of the justice alphabet. One could anticipate the vowel status of happiness from its importance in the three traditional formulas. Happiness can combine with any other value and always appears as one of the letters in a justice sentence. Liberty also may combine with any other value; it usually appears in both the production and distribution words. H and L are the vowels in the justice alphabet. All the other letters are the consonants.

These justice letters are then combined to form justice words. For example, equality, happiness, and liberty might be combined to form the word EHL. The appearance of this word in a principle of distributive justice would tell us that in the distribution in question, the values of equality, happiness, and liberty should be achieved. Obviously, a large number of such words could be constructed. The number of words in a language depends on the number and kind of sentences needed to perform adequately the task of communication.

Spelling rules. Not any combination of letters can be put together to form a word. For example, in the English language q is always followed by u. It is a rule that u always follows q. Such rules are required in the justice alphabet as well. Not every combination of values is appropriate. Just as the rules for spelling rule out certain combinations of letters, the spelling rules of justice rule out certain value combinations. Such rules eliminate some possibilities for distributive justice regardless of the society's economic situation. A justice sentence contains three kinds of words in the following order:

Production word   Economic word   Distribution word

The choice of these words and the order in which they appear in the sentence will be defended later. Our present task is to provide some spelling rules for the various words. The spelling rules for principles of justice are given and explained below.

F_1: Every distribution word must contain the vowel H.

The force of this rule is to make happiness a necessary condition of distributive justice. If a distribution is to be considered just, some happiness must always be achieved in distribution.

F_2: O must always be followed by A.

The force of this rule is to show the connection between optimization (effi-

20. Plato, *The Sophist,* trans. F. M. Cornford, in *Collected Dialogues,* ed. Hamilton and Cairns (New York: Random House, Inc., 1963), pp. 998-9.

ciency) and ability. A productive system is not optimized unless everyone is doing what he has the ability to do, that is, what he can do best. This rule does require a qualification, however. In any productive system, certain abilities may not be utilized because they are either socially undesirable or because there is no demand for them. Hence, the rule that efficiency demands that everyone does his best is qualified to apply only when the productive tasks are both acceptable and in demand.

F_3: M does not appear in the second word of the principles of distributive justice.

The force of this rule is to deny that the distribution which results naturally as the result of the productive system is either just or morally right. The economic distribution is not necessarily the just distribution.

F_4: The letter E is always followed by a vowel; it is followed by either H or L.

This rule has resulted from my analysis of egalitarianism in Chapter III. It denies that equality is a vowel and can combine with any value. More importantly, it denies that equality independently determines just distributions. Equality is relevant when the concern is with equal rights. Equality always combines with either happiness or liberty to form the syllables EL and EH. These syllables represent the equal right to liberty and the equal right to a minimum standard of living.

Syntax rules. Our first syntax rule concerns the type of words that must appear in any well-formed justice sentence.

S_1: Each justice sentence must contain a production word, an economic income word, and a distribution word.

Our second syntax rule concerns the order of these words.

S_2: All words of the complete justice sentence must be arranged in the following order: Production word   Economic word   Distribution word

In S_2 the first word in the principle refers to those values which should be achieved in production. The second word provides the link between the production word and the distribution word. H represents the potential value of happiness from the economic income produced by the economic system. The third word refers to those values achieved in the just distribution of income. This just distribution is achieved by redistributing economic income so that certain values are achieved. At any given time, the amount of economic income equals the amount of just income but the distribution is different.

S_1 is justified since just income is causally dependent on production and the resulting economic income; our first attention should be directed to the values one seeks to achieve in production. The kind of productive system we create determines the options we have for just income. It is ridiculous to utilize principles of distribution relevant to a society of scarcity when the productive capacity is that of a society of affluence. Furthermore, this word order steers the social philosopher in the right direction. The just distribution of income is best achieved by a redistribution of economic income rather than by a complicated and detailed planning of the productive process.

The justification of S_2 can be seen when we consider the nature of language. In English at least, the words must be in a certain order if they are to constitute a sentence. For example, "cat boy the hit the" is not a sentence while "The boy hit the cat" is a sentence. Similarly the value combinations which constitute words of principles of distributive justice cannot be arranged in any order. S_2 provides the appropriate ordering rule.

Having established the correct word order for the principles, further spelling rules can be provided.

F_5: The first word of the principle must contain either the syllable EL or OA.

Every productive system must either be efficient or provide an equal right to liberty.

F_6: The second and third words always contain H.

Happiness is a necessary condition of distribution whether the distribution be natural or just.

Translation of "justice language." Some instructions are required for translating the justice language into English. Recall that each letter of the justice alphabet represents a value. The production and distribution words of justice sentences tell us what values ought to be realized in production and distribution.

As in English, the words of the justice language may contain several syllables. Certain letters combine together, and in some cases must combine together, to form syllables. Our discussion in Chapter III successfully argued that one seeks to achieve equality in distributive justice only in the context of achieving equal rights. In the justice language our equal right to liberty will be symbolized by the syllable EL. When EL appears in the production word it refers to negative liberty, specifically our right to choose our occupation free from coercion. When EL appears in the distribution word it refers to positive liberty, specifically the equal right to equal opportunity. In the justice language our equal right to a certain standard of living is symbolized by the syllable EH.

In addition the order of the letters or syllables is most important as well. The first letter or syllable indicates the value that has priority. Hence if one sees the word EL-OA in the production spot of the principles, he would know that in this situation the just productive system is the one which is organized efficiently to the extent compatible with everyone's right to liberty. Efficiency and freedom of occupation are the values to be achieved with freedom of occupation receiving priority. Similarly if EH-EL should appear in the distribution spot, this word would tell us that economic income should be distributed so that the equal rights to happiness and liberty are achieved. This means specifically that the just redistribution of money income should achieve a minimum standard of living and equal freedom of opportunity for all.

We can illustrate the entire procedure by considering the following principle:

$$OA\text{-}EL \qquad H \qquad EH\text{-}EL$$

This principle tells us that in this situation the just distributive system is as follows: Production should be organized as efficiently as possible and that one should have freedom of occupation so long as it is consistent with efficiency. The word order shows that efficiency has priority. The second word, H, is the same for all principles. It refers to the happiness which can result from the natural distribution of the productive system. It provides the raw material which is then redistributed so that a minimum standard of living and equal opportunity is provided for all.

5. The Principles of Distributive Justice

At this point it may be appropriate to summarize our results thus far.

MODEL	THING MODELLED
1. The model is the construction of principles for communicating in a language well.	1. The thing modelled is the construction of principles for achieving a just economic system.
2. The basic elements of the model are letters.	2. The basic elements of the thing modelled are values.
3. Spelling (formation) rules give instructions for combining letters into words.	3. Spelling (formation) rules give instructions for combining values into justice words.
4. Syntax rules enable us to combine the words into well-formed sentences.	4. Syntax rules enable us to combine the justice words into well-formed principles.

Our remaining task is by far the most important one. It is at this point that we relate our justice language to the world. We must supply the context rules for each of our economic systems. What I now propose is to use the rules to resolve the competing value claims, i.e., I see the problem of distributive justice as Rawls and Rescher do, but I am seeking to resolve it in a way different from Rawls. In effect, I will now provide the substantive principles of distributive justice. Each of the following rules are to be understood in terms of the following formula:

When faced with economic situation S, achieve distributive justice by following rule *r*.

Extreme scarcity. In a situation of extreme scarcity, the complete principle of distributive justice is as follows:

$$P_1: \qquad OA \qquad H \qquad EHOA\text{-}EHM$$

This principle states that in a situation of extreme scarcity, production should be as efficient as possible. The produced goods should then be redistributed so that the producers are provided a minimum standard of living. If goods remain, the remainder should be distributed so as to provide a minimum standard of living for those who possess some accepted M characteristics. In this case M might be as basic as being a woman or child. Those who are neither producers nor possess the M characteristic are allowed to perish.

This principle seems sound because the society must struggle to provide conditions of survival for anyone. Since some must perish it is imperative to keep this number as small as possible. This is done by making the productive system as efficient as possible. In such a situation one does not have a right to choose his occupation. The resulting goods should be distributed to the point where the producers achieve a minimum standard of living. No producer is entitled to more than a minimum standard of living so long as it is possible to keep others alive. Any goods which remain after the provision of a minimum standard of living to the producers should go towards providing a minimum standard of living for others, using an accepted M characteristic (s) as a criterion.

Minimum standard of living. The appropriate formula for a society in a subsistence situation is as follows:

$$P_2: \qquad OA \qquad H \qquad EH$$

The appropriate principle, like the society, closely resembles the extreme situation. However, we need no longer restrict our distribution of the minimum standard of living to the producers and the possessors of some M characteristics. Fortunately this society is able to produce enough for all to remain alive.

However, no one is entitled to more than a minimum standard of living since a greater share for some would effect loss of life for others. It is assumed that all those who can work do so. It is also assumed that the rather extensive process of redistribution will not adversely affect incentives to production. This assumption is not a large one provided it is clear that the situation is so serious that an extra share for some would cause the death of another. Most people do make extensive sacrifices in such situations. The assumption is most reasonable in a small society—the society, in fact, where this situation is most likely to occur. However, the practical problem is serious indeed, in the large underdeveloped countries whose productive capacities lay between scarcity and comfort. Shortly, this problem will be discussed at length.

The comfortable society. Another principle of distributive justice is required for an economic system that can provide a minimum standard of decency for all. In such a society the appropriate principle of distributive justice can be provisionally stated as follows:

Provisional P_3:   EL-OA   H   EH-EL

Such a level of productive capacity marks a turning point in distributive justice. Liberty, both positive and negative, becomes an important value to be achieved. At the same time the value of efficiency becomes less important. This inverse relation between the two values continues as the society becomes more affluent. In the comfortable society, on the production side the equal right to choose one's occupation has priority. What makes this freedom significant, however, are the values one achieves in the final distribution of income. Negative freedom of occupation is enhanced because the job applicant is not concerned with salary differentials. Everyone is guaranteed a minimum standard of decency and there is no surplus to provide income differentials. In this society, the final distribution radically affects the traditional right to choose one's occupation. Freedom of occupation is constrained only by natural ability. In this case, negative and positive liberty work together to provide significance to one's freedom to choose his occupation. In the comfortable society everyone has the job which he enjoys most, given his ability and qualifications. Whichever choice he makes, he is guaranteed a minimum standard of decency.

Unfortunately, this principle creates serious practical problems. Such a principle would destroy incentives and reduce efficiency. The principle seems to undermine the pricing system which allocates scarce resources, and the egalitarian implications of redistribution would seem to undermine incentives. In general, the principle is open to the charge of being unrealistic and utopian. Problems of incentive and efficiency occur at three points. First, without an effective wage differential, there would be serious shortages in some occupations and serious overcrowding in others. In other words, there would be severe distortions in the labor market. Secondly, it is alleged that the required extensive redistribution of economic income would destroy incentive. Thirdly, why should we assume that the goods and services which provide a minimum standard of decency are the ones which are most desired by consumers? Perhaps consumers would rather spend the extra income on household conveniences or elaborate clothing. If the desires of the consumers diverge from the requirements for a minimum standard of decency, a dilemma results. Either consumer sovereignty must be violated or consumer sovereignty will be maintained and freedom of opportunity will not be achieved. For these three reasons it may be argued that provisional P_3 is unworkable.

The concept of a minimum standard of decency and some modifications in the principle may provide an escape from these difficulties. First, with respect to the allocation of labor, wage differentials are not the only means for allocation. In the first place, job qualifications and differences in natural ability will provide considerable natural allocation. One must be qualified to be a surgeon. Secondly, differences in taste will provide further natural allocation. In fact this aspect of natural allocation will be strengthened because choice of occupation will not depend on salary considerations. I do not pretend, however, that these two devices can completely replace the pricing system. Fortunately, the provision of a minimum standard of decency does allow for wage differentials. There are a large number of constitutents of equal opportunity. Education, social security, medical insurance, unemployment insurance, etc., are all elements of a minimum standard of decency. A society does not achieve a minimum standard of decency in one step; some elements are achieved and then others are achieved. This piecemeal process of achievement enables one to provide wage differentials. As a new element is introduced it will first be provided in those occupations where shortages exist in order to induce laborers into that occupation. Hence, as any element of positive liberty is provided, it will first be distributed on the basis of efficiency and will act as a pricing mechanism. Gradually this element of positive liberty will be provided to all, and a new element will be introduced on efficiency grounds. An example illustrates this procedure. Let us assume that a high school education and medical insurance are available to all. Everyone has an equal right to these commodities. However, those occupations which need more laborers might offer such features as paid vacations and college education for employee children in order to attract employees. The point is that freedom of opportunity is not something to which everyone has an equal right all at once. One has an equal right to part of it; the rest is introduced on the basis of efficiency, i.e., on the basis of the market. Hence the third word of P_3 can be modified to express this fact. The just distribution is made in accordance with EH-LOA-EL. In this way, the minimum standard of decency is broken up into two parts. Everyone has an equal right to some aspects; others are awarded on efficiency grounds.

Incentives. The second problem is the effect of redistribution on incentives. First, the considerations above have introduced some differentiation into income distribution. This will enable those who receive more economic income to have more just income as well, and hence the adverse affect on incentive will be reduced. Secondly, if the assumption is made that most people enjoy doing what they are able to do, we are assured that everyone is reasonably happy with his job. This is a great boost to incentive. Job satisfaction is important, and even if a man loses much of his economic income in redistribution, job satisfaction will provide incentive. Thirdly, nonmonetary incentives can be used. Such nonmonetary incentives can be effective, as the cooperative programs of Scandinavian countries illustrate. Nonmonetary incentives may play an even larger role in the future.

Should someone argue that the incentive problem is still not resolved, I can only say that if he is correct, what is just and what is right part company. It may be right to concede to greed so that the economy will not move backward to subsistence, but it is not just. I doubt, however, that those who challenge this view can give a convincing argument based on empirical evidence that such a concession is necessary.[21]

The third problem focuses on freedom of opportunity and consumer sovereignty. How do we know that people desire the goods and services required for freedom of opportunity and hence that they will be produced? Again the broad concept of a minimum standard of decency helps here. Certainly, there is no difficulty with condition (a), the minimum standard of living. The goods and services required for a minimum standard of living do in fact have first priority in the list of consumer preferences.

The basic problem centers around condition (b), more specifically around the scientific aspects of condition (b). For example, freedom from ignorance and insecurity are desires of almost everyone. However, are these desires next in the order of priority after the desire for a minimum standard of living? Although we can say that people do desire medical and unemployment insurance, education, recreational facilities, and cultural opportunities, and although we can also say that these or similar goods do provide freedom from ignorance and insecurity and hence freedom of opportunity, we cannot determine the exact extent of the desire for them. Most of these goods are

21. An excellent article on incentives which includes reference to empirical research is George F. Break "The Effects of Taxation on Work Incentives" in *Private Wants and Public Needs,* ed. Edmund S. Phelps (New York: W. W. Norton & Company, Inc., 1965), pp. 55–65.

public goods and hence the actual desire for them is not reflected in the marketplace.[22] Moreover, in actual societies further distortion of preferences has resulted because noninformational advertising has induced desires for other goods and services before freedom of opportunity has been provided for all. Whatever the actual situation, the priority of freedom of opportunity for the realization of other values requires that the goods and services required for freedom of opportunity be produced regardless of consumer demand. Hence these goods are merit goods and the letter M must be added to the production word in P_3. There are numerous reasons to believe that the addition of M to the formula does not interfere with consumer sovereignty to any great extent. First, freedom of opportunity and the goods and services required for obtaining it may in fact represent the order of priority of consumers. Secondly, the possibility that provision of freedom of opportunity accurately represents consumer desire is enhanced if the distorting influences of noninformational advertising for luxury goods are omitted. This distortion has been discussed by many economists, but has received its most popular treatment by John Kenneth Galbraith.[23] Thirdly, government provision for public goods enhances the satisfaction of consumer desires rather than hinders them. Fourthly, even if consumer sovereignty with respect to production is violated in certain cases, consumer sovereignty over income is retained. The consumer still may choose from the variety of educational, recreational, and cultural goods and services which are produced.[24] Fifthly, there is no conflict with consumer sovereignty with respect to the nonscientific aspects of condition (b) nor with condition (c). The only government interference with consumer market demand in these areas is to provide for public goods.

This detailed discussion should assure us that the priority given to freedom of opportunity and the addition of M to the production word does not undermine P_3. It can now be restated as follows:

$$P_3: \quad EL\text{-}M\text{-}OA \quad H \quad EH\text{-}LOA\text{-}EL .$$

This principle does avoid the threefold objection concerning practicability which has been raised against provisional P_3. Finally, it is assumed that no one wastes the goods and services society provides for freedom of opportunity. If we drop this assumption, justice demands that after some point,

22. The reader is referred to note 36 of Chapter II for the vast literature on this subject.
23. John Kenneth Galbraith, *The Affluent Society* (New York: Mentor Books, 1958). See also Tibor Scitovsky, *Papers on Welfare and Growth,* Section C "Practical Welfare Economics" (Stanford: Stanford University Press, 1964), pp. 193–272.
24. This central planning does not diminish freedom to any appreciable extent. This point is well argued by Barbara Wootton, *Freedom Under Planning* (Chapel Hill: University of North Carolina Press, 1945). See esp. chap. 4.

the individual forfeits his right to positive liberty. I do not tnink the cutoff point can be determined theoretically, but the poorer the society the lower the cutoff point should be. The earlier cutoff point is required because efficiency is so much more important in a poorer society. A poor society cannot and ought not absorb the waste that a wealthier society can absorb.

Affluence. The productive capacity of the affluent society is enormous. In such a society the principle of just distribution is as follows:

$$P_4: \quad EL\text{-}M\text{-}OA \quad H \quad EH\text{-}EL\text{-}HOA$$

In the affluent society, the value of efficiency is decidedly subordinate. The productive output of the affluent society is so great that a large amount of inefficiency can be sustained. Ironically, however, P_4 still creates much smaller problems with respect to efficiency and incentives than was the case with P_3. The sheer magnitude of the goods and services alleviates the problem. Even after a minimum standard of decency is provided for all, a substantial amount of goods and services remain. This excess may be kept by those who receive it naturally from the workings of the marketplace. After a minimum standard of decency has been provided, economic income and just income are the same. The fact that the excess income goes to those who receive it through the market is reflected in the third syllable of the distribution word, HOA. The affluent society presents a fortunate situation since we have the same freedom of occupational choice as in the comfortable society and also wage differentials to aid efficiency as well. The laborer has four alternatives. Ideally, he would have a job which he both enjoys and which provides an income in excess of a minimum standard of decency. At the worst, his ability may limit him to a job which he does not greatly enjoy and he will receive no income in excess of a minimum standard of decency. In the middle some will choose higher salaries over complete job satisfaction while others will choose complete job satisfaction over higher salaries. In no case, however, need anyone receive an income below a minimum standard of decency.

Consideration of the affluent society provides an excellent opportunity to discuss one further aspect of merit goods. Our discussion of positive liberty in the comfortable society has already indicated the responsibility of government for providing the means to freedom of opportunity in particular and for public goods in general. The achievement of freedom of opportunity for all and the increasing supply of additional goods and services in the affluent society creates one further problem which must be taken into account. What consideration should be given to minority tastes, i.e., to those tastes which a minority finds desirable, but which a market economy would not fulfill? For example, assume that the cost of building and maintaining an FM radio station exceeds the income that would be received from advertising and donations. In a competitive market economy, the FM station would not be built.

The minority FM listeners could argue that the FM station should be treated as a merit good and hence that it should be built even though this creates some disturbance with consumer demand. The station might be financed by a 10 percent tax on popular records. On the other hand, the majority popular-record buyer will certainly argue that FM stations do not deserve special attention. Either the FM listener should sacrifice enough of his other goods and services to allow the station to be built or there should be no FM stations.

The FM listener has two appropriate rejoinders. First, the economic situation is analogous to the political situation. A political system is not just simply because it provides each man with a vote. If an unchanging minority is outvoted by an unchanging majority on every issue and if minority preferences are completely ignored, the political system is not just. *Mutatis mutandis* such an economic system is not just either. It is not part of the principles of distributive justice that majority interests completely determine the production of any particular kind of good. Secondly, the amount of goods and services that the FM listener may have to sacrifice to pay for the FM station may be excessive. Certainly, the FM listeners should sacrifice something, but they should not have to sacrifice so much that condition (c) of a minimum standard of decency is violated, i.e., their sacrifice for an FM station should not create an excessive income differential between themselves and the rest of society. The exact amount of the sacrifice that should be exacted from the FM listeners cannot be determined in the abstract. However, as a guideline, the greater the extent of the satisfaction of the majority, the less the minority should have to sacrifice. For example, the sacrifice of the FM listeners should be less if there are ten AM stations serving the area than it would be if there were only two. For these reasons at least some goods which satisfy minority taste should be treated as merit goods and produced in excess of market demand.

Finally, a brief remark must be made about the partial coincidence of economic income and just income. Some might argue that after a minimum standard of decency has been achieved, the remaining money income should be redistributed according to some finer principles. I reject this approach because a minimum standard of decency, in my opinion, marks the limit for setting up principles of distributive justice for the economic system as a whole. To try to set up a more precise standard would certainly create all the practical difficulties which plague the socialist formula. After a minimum standard of decency is achieved, the interests of justice are best served by letting economic income and just income coincide. In these cases "to each according to what the market provides" seems appropriate. Moreover, should the inequality become excessive, the violation of condition (c) of a minimum standard of decency would require further redistribution.

Intermediate societies. Unfortunately, actual societies do not always fit into the neat classification provided above. Many societies are between subsistence and comfort or between comfort and affluence.

If the society lies between subsistence and comfort, the following principle of distributive justice is appropriate:

$$P_5: \quad OA\text{-}EL \quad H \quad EH\text{-}LOA$$

Since there is a surplus of goods beyond a minimum standard of living, these goods should be distributed on the basis of market efficiency. Since we have entered the first stages of a minimum standard of decency, it is consistent with our discussion of efficiency and incentives that the initial elements be awarded on the basis of the market. This is especially necessary to help mitigate the severe practical problems caused by redistribution in underdeveloped economies. After a minimum standard of living has been provided, the just income coincides with economic income. The benefits of positive liberty are distributed according to the market up to that point where P_3 can be applied, that is, up to that point where some elements of positive liberty can be applied to all.

On the production side, the value of equal liberty to choose one's occupation is added. Efficiency still has priority, however.

If the society is between comfort and affluence, the following principle will provide distributive justice:

$$P_6: \quad EL\text{-}M\text{-}OA \quad H \quad EH\text{-}EL\text{-}LOA$$

The principle for this intermediate society differs little from that of a comfortable society. In distribution, EL and LOA have changed positions. This alteration shows clearly that the society has moved beyond the first stages in the provision of a minimum standard of decency. However, some aspects of a minimum standard of decency are still determined by the marketplace.

Economic growth. Until now nothing has been said about the progress of a society from a condition of extreme scarcity or subsistence to a condition of affluence. Much of the analysis of this complicated question lies beyond the scope of philosophy. However, since some present consumption is often sacrificed for increased future consumption and since the sacrifice of present consumption in underdeveloped countries creates a special hardship, the moral philosopher cannot ignore the problem altogether.

The moral philosopher can make a few general comments, however. First, it seems certain that the rate of growth of a society which follows the principles of justice above will be slower than that of one in which a large segment of the population is kept at subsistence level or worse. Principles of justice would not sanction the ruthless exploitation of the present for a more rapid economic growth. Secondly, until a society reaches the point where P_3 can be applied, most of the growth will occur from investments in labor and technological discovery. In such underdeveloped countries even the most elementary technical discoveries may be of great importance for growth. Moreover, as workers first obtain improved food, clothing, and shelter, and then security from accident, adequate health treatment, and job security, the productivity of labor will rise. In addition, provisions for education provide investment for growth as well as freedom of opportunity. Again, this may not be the quickest way to achieve economic growth in these societies, but it is the most just. Finally, once a society reaches the point where P_3 can be applied, provision can be made for capital investment. The amount withheld for investment should be considered a merit good and is represented by M in the production word in formulas P_3, P_4, and P_6. The exact amount to be withheld varies, but it should not be so much as to interfere with either the laborer's minimum standard of living, or with education and technological discovery. As society becomes more affluent, provision for growth becomes less important.

This brief discussion should indicate that none of the formulas presented above impede economic growth to the extent that societies will stagnate in one position. An orderly and just rate of growth will occur when the formulas above are applied to the relevant society. It is admitted, however, that the rate of growth will be more gradual in these societies than in those where present citizens are deliberately exploited to provide for the future.

Distributive justice in limited situations. Problems of distributive justice are not limited to the problem of the just economic system. There are also problems of distributing family income, local shortages, and temporary overcrowding. If my theory of distributive justice is to be comprehensive, it must have something to say in these situations as well. In most cases, the principles above can be adapted rather easily. In the limited cases, the production word of the principle does not apply. In these situations one starts with a limited amount and then proceeds to distribute or redistribute it. To do this the limited situation is classified in one of the six ways above. The distribution word of the principle for that classification will usually give the correct solution. For this reason, I speak of the principles applied in limited situations as the application of elliptical principles. In grammar some sentences do not have any subjects. Commands often exhibit this property, e.g., "Be good," "Close the door," and "No parking." With such sentences we speak of the subject as being understood. In each of the above commands, "you" is understood to be the subject. In certain situations we are not concerned with the justice of an entire economic system. In such cases the values in the production word are taken for granted and ignored just as the "you" in commands.

The distribution of family income illustrates this approach exactly. If the family income is one of extreme scarcity, the appropriate distribution is EHOA-EHM. If the living conditions fall below the minimum standard, each of the providers has an equal right to the minimum and if there is anything remaining, the further distribution is made on the basis of some M characteristic(s). If the subsistence income is a family's lot, the distribution should be made on the basis of EH. Every person has an equal right to the minimum standard. This standard can just be met. Once a family's income reaches a standard of comfort, the appropriate distribution is given by EH-LOA-EL. Each member of the family achieves some level of positive liberty. In this limited situation LOA has a slightly different meaning, however. Although the reference is still to the values of efficiency and ability, the reference is not to market efficiency. This elliptical principle can be illustrated by considering a traditional problem of distributive justice. Suppose a man can send some of his sons to college but not all of them, or suppose that he could send them all only by sacrificing the extended educational requirements of a medical degree for his gifted son. The second syllable LOA provides the clue for a solution. In both cases the decision should be made on the basis of ability if such a discrimination is possible. The letter O rightly raises the question of efficiency. The older children should go first once discrimination according to ability has been made. The older children will then be able to assist the education of their younger brothers and/or the family situation will change in the meantime. In the case of the medical student, the age of the parties involved will also help determine justice. So long as the medical student is not substantially older, his brothers can finish their education and then subsidize their talented brother's medical education. If the medical student is older, he can subsidize his younger brothers. What is required is to find the variables, such as age, which will enable the greatest amount of education for the least cost. This is the instruction which LOA provides.

In the affluent family, the appropriate distribution is EH-EL-HOA. Again however, the syllable HOA has a different meaning in this context. If the parallel with the affluent society were followed exactly, all money in excess of a minimum standard of decency would belong to the breadwinner. In the affluent society, the excess belongs to those who have received it naturally from the workings of the economic system. Hence, in the family situation, the breadwinner would have it all. This would not be just. In this case the syllable HOA instructs the family unit to maximize happiness. The family can make those finer discriminations of need which representatives of society as a whole cannot make. Hence, it is able to redistribute the extra income on the basis of some criteria which are not available to society. For example, in the abstract we can say that recreation is an element of a decent standard of living. However, condition (c) of a minimum standard of living is the only basis for an estimate of the amount and kind of recreation required. The family, however, can make fine discriminations within the family structure. For example, if James collects rare postage stamps and John makes model airplanes, extra money for James's more costly postage stamps is certainly justified. After a minimum standard of living is achieved, HOA instructs the family to make those fine discriminations which will enable it to provide the greatest happiness for the greatest number.

For families which fall into the intermediary classifications, the distribution words of those principles do provide distributive justice utilizing the type of analysis provided above.

To solve each particular problem which might arise is a task whose magnitude is too great to consider here. My own thinking and the analysis of the limited situations above lead me to adopt the following rule for the limited cases:

Rule for limited cases: Place the limited cases into one of the six classifications. Then utilize the principle for that classification by taking the distribution word of that principle and use it to make the distribution so that the values in that word are achieved.

The fit may not be exact for each case, but the rule does provide a general principle for distributive justice in the limited situation.

Summary. A brief summary of the six principles of distributive justice and some observations based on these principles is now in order. In the final section, I shall attempt a general assessment of the overall theory.

A. Extreme scarcity	P_1: OA	H	EHOA-EHM
B. Subsistence:	P_2: OA	H	EH
C. Comfort:	P_3: EL-M-OA	H	EH-LOA-EL
D. Affluence:	P_4: EL-M-OA	H	EH-EL-HOA
E. Subsistence/comfort:	P_5: OA-EL	H	EH-LOA
F. Comfort/affluence:	P_6: EL-M-OA	H	EH-EL-LOA

As one surveys the principles above, some rather interesting conclusions can be drawn. First, as one moves toward affluence, the achievement of distributive justice coincides with the achievement of the good society. In fact, liberty depends for its realization on rising living standards as the principles illustrate. As the living standards rise, freedom of occupation becomes a significant right. Regardless of the occupation one chooses, he has the security of an adequate standard of decency. In addition, increased productivity enables us to put more emphasis on merit goods and services and to make certain that minority tastes have some influence in the market. In this way liberty expands as productivity expands. In general, as one moves from subsistence to affluence, efficiency loses priority and liberty both expands in meaning and gains in priority.

Secondly, the greatest practical problems occur in the more underdeveloped economies. The conflict between efficiency in production and the other values in distribution is more acute. To overcome poverty an extremely efficient economic system is required. The distribution of economic income such a system produces, however, is highly unequal. If this inequality is maintained, a most fundamental human right to a minimum standard of living cannot be achieved. Some live in luxury while others survive on a subsistence level at best. Redistribution is obviously required, yet the redistribution must not be so extensive that efficiency is reduced; the poor society cannot afford inefficiency. My principles are designed to mitigate this conflict as much as possible.

Thirdly, a brief word must be provided about the emotional issue of economic liberty or consumer sovereignty. In general I allow for three types of economic liberty. First, a man usually has the right to choose his occupation without suffering extreme economic deprivation. Secondly, as the productive capacity of a society increases, a man has a right to positive liberty, i.e., to those conditions which provide him the freedom of opportunity to achieve his goals and develop his abilities. Finally, a man has consumer sovereignty with respect to his just income. He can spend it as he pleases. With certain merit goods, however, some citizens surrender some consumer sovereignty over production. The liberty which I do deny throughout is that a man is free to spend all his economic income as he pleases. A man does not necessarily have a right to his total economic income. The distribution of the marketplace is not the just distribution. Of course, I am not saying that he does not have a moral right to any of his economic income nor am I saying that economic income and just income do not coincide in any respects.

6. Assessment of the Theory

The principles of distributive justice developed above may seem unsatisfactory for the following reasons. Some might argue that my classification of societies is too broad. Hence my six principles expressed by the context rules would be too broad. Some might argue that I should be more concerned with international economic justice than with the economic systems of various states. Some might argue that I have provided no reasons for accepting my rules.

The classification of societies. Perhaps the best way to consider the charge that my classification of societies is too broad is to return to the language model. In this way, I think we will see that such an objection can be met. The following analogy can be made. Just as men do not discriminate between every possible state of affairs and just as the languages of men do not have separate words to apply to each possible state of affairs, men cannot conceive of all possible circumstances which might distinguish one society from another. Any such attempt would be impracticable and uneconomical. Hence my classification of societies and my corresponding justice principles are based on the same kinds of practical considerations that we utilize in classifying states of affairs and in constructing a language to describe them.

My opponent may grant that the classification of societies cannot be complete, but he might deny that my classification is sufficiently detailed. This dispute could be endless. I can only say that my classification does encompass the major types of economic systems and that I have developed justice principles for each. Moreover, these principles are not otiose. By using them, present economic systems can be indicted on several counts.

Should even this not satisfy my critic, another approach can be taken. A language can build up words and sentences as they are needed for finer discriminations of states of affairs. There is no reason why the principles of distributive justice cannot be built up in this way as well. Even if the critic does not accept my classification, he can use my approach to make his own classification and to develop his own corresponding principles. However, my own feeling is that I have provided plausible principles of distributive justice which can be used as flexible guides and which can be expanded easily in more complicated situations. This seems to be precisely what the situation demands.

International economic justice. The objection might be raised that the account above makes no reference to international economic justice. What obligations does a country in a state of affluence owe to a country at the subsistence level? If the answer could be based solely on distributive justice, the principles above could be applied with ease. The six principles would not refer to different nations at the same time but to all nations at different times. A commitment to international economic justice would mean that the wealth of the rich nations would be redistributed to all citizens of the world so that they receive a minimum standard of living and then a minimum standard of decency. All that is required is to ascertain the economic situation of the world as a whole and then apply the relevant principle on the whole. The principles are sound when applied to the world as a whole, but the international situation makes their application impractical. In the present situation, what possible motives could be used to convince Americans to return to a minimum standard of decency in order to substantially raise the living standards of the Chinese or the Africans?

The usual difficulties of redistribution become impossible obstacles when nationalism is a relevant variable. Something must be done to lessen the gap between rich and poor, but the gap cannot be closed on moral principles of distributive justice alone. Questions of politics and psychology must play a part. In order to avoid these complexities, I have limited my principles of distributive justice to national economic systems. However, if the considerations are limited to distributive justice, the six principles can apply to the world as a whole. In fact, my principles or their elliptical counterparts apply to the world as a whole, to national economies, or to limited situations.

Why these principles? One can demand justification for accepting these principles of distributive justice rather than some others. It is here that the features of the language model do not carry over. The justification for the rules of a language seem pragmatic. My justification for the principles espoused in this chapter is that they meet the conditions established in Chapter I. They do not fall victim to obvious counterexamples. The reasons for this become fairly clear when you compare my theory against its rivals. In general these reasons can be summed up by the words flexibility, multiplicity, and practicability.

Flexibility. The language model provides an ideal solution for the problems of lack of flexibility which infect many of the traditional theories. We can expand and modify our rules as conditions change. This theory is not synoptic the way philosophical utilitarianism and Rawls's social contract theory are. Unlike philosophical utilitarianism, it is not necessary to calculate an indefinite number of future consequences in order to determine what is just or unjust. Unlike Rawls's view, it is not necessary to try to define a just procedure once and for all. There is no need to plan or to specify the institutions and procedures for a just society in great detail. Hence, I have tried to avoid the methodological difficulties which Braybrooke and Lindblom have so convincingly pressed against the synoptic approach.

Multiplicity. Using the language model, it is easy to resist the temptation to try to construct *one* principle of distributive justice which can apply in all situations. It is just this mistake that dooms the traditional theories. It is also easy to resist the temptation to make the opposite error and believe that an intuitive judgment is necessary for each situation.

In the second place, my principles utilize a fairly large number of concepts. In the traditional theories, only a few concepts are used and there is a tendency to stretch these concepts too far. The utilitarians use happiness to cover a wide range of human experience. In the egalitarian theory it is the equal right to well-being which causes the difficulty. The concept of well-being may be limited to a minimum standard of living or it may be expanded to include complete well-being. However, once you move beyond a minimum standard of living, it is very difficult to determine the level of well-being to which everyone has an equal right. Finally, in the socialist theory, the concept of need is stretched too far. Distribution according to need works very well when limited to basic needs and certain nonbasic needs such as education and security against accident and unemployment. However, the principle breaks down when there are a large number of goods and services to be distributed because it is impossible to determine which needs are most urgent.

Another advantage of my principles is the multiplicity of values utilized. Unlike the traditional theories, no relevant values are ruled out. For example, in economic utilitarianism those abilities not in demand may receive a very inadequate remuneration. In most of my principles, everyone is provided a minimum; no classical musician would fall below a minimum standard of decency. In socialism, no provision is made for exceptional ability; in my theory there is such a provision. I have also attempted to take account of the many kinds of liberty and to give each of them a place in the principles. The only value which has not been emphasized in this chapter is that aspect of merit which refers to the personal characteristics of the recipients. All the principles above rest on the assumptions that all able people provide some contribution to the productive effort and that no one abuses his right to a minimum standard of living or his right to freedom of opportunity. We could drop this assumption, however, and add M to EH and EL in all distribution words.

Practicability. The theory based on the language model is a practical moral theory in the sense that it is not designed for a society of angels. Our basic moral intuitions as well as certain facts about human desire and motivation are taken into account. I have tried to do better with respect to unrealistic assumptions than economic utilitarianism. However, the principles provided are moral principles and if they are to be followed, men must not be solely rational egoists. The principles are designed for moral men.

Secondly, I do not require an unrealistic degree of specificity for my theory. In other words, I think it is a mistake to apply the mathematical model to the problem of distributive justice. Problems of distributive justice do not fit readily into a quantitative framework. The utilitarian theories fail on just this ground. Concepts such as happiness and welfare are too vague for precise mathematical analysis. Moreover, the problems of distributive justice are not analogous to scientific laws for all the reasons that contemporary meta-ethical theories indicate. Moral laws have a different function from scientific laws.

Thirdly, the important role that production must play in any theory of distributive justice is clearly recognized. Implied in this context is a recognition of the value of efficiency in production. This recognition avoids one of the major difficulties of philosophical utilitarianism and all forms of egalitarianism. All my principles contain a production word and the position of the word in the principles indicates its importance.

Finally, the flexibility of a theory of distributive justice based on the language model adds to its practicability. The language model illuminates the process for constructing principles of distributive justice and shows how a complex theory might be built up. It is this feature of the theory which enables me to say that a step towards a new theory of distributive justice has been provided.

In conclusion, I have tried to provide a set of principles of distributive justice. The problem of distributive justice is to apply and order the relevant values in scarcity situations. I have used the language model to show how this might be done and how it can be continually done in more complex situations.

Bibliography

Books

Arrow, Kenneth J. *Social Choice and Individual Values.* Second edition. New York: John Wiley & Sons, 1963.

Bator, Francis M. *The Question of Government Spending.* New York: Collier Books, 1960.

Baumol, William J. *Welfare Economics and the Theory of the State.* Second edition. Cambridge: Harvard University Press, 1965.

Benn, Stanley and R. S. Peters. *Principles of Political Thought.* New York: Collier Books, 1959.

Bentham, Jeremy. *Principles of Morals and Legislation.* In *The Utilitarians.* Garden City, New York: Doubleday & Company, Inc., 1961.

_____. *Constitutional Code. Works,* Vol. 9. Edited by John Bowring. New York: Russell and Russell, 1962.

Bergson, Abram. *Essays In Normative Economics.* Cambridge: Harvard University Press, 1966.

Boulding, Kenneth E. *Principles of Economic Policy.* Englewood Cliffs, New Jersey: Prentice-Hall Inc., 1958.

Braithwaite, Richard. *Theory of Games As A Tool For The Moral Philosopher.* Cambridge: Cambridge University Press, 1955.

Brandt, Richard (ed.). *Social Justice.* Englewood Cliffs, New Jersey: Prentice-Hall Inc., 1962.

Braybrooke, David and Charles E. Lindblom. *A Strategy of Decision.* New York: The Free Press, 1963.

Buchanan, James M. and Gordon Tullock. *The Calculus of Consent.* Ann Arbor: University of Michigan Press, 1962.

Chapman, John and J. Roland Pennock (eds.). *Nomos IX Equality.* New York: Atherton Press, 1967.

Childs, Marquis. *Sweeden: The Middle Way.* New Haven: Yale University Press, 1936.

Crosland, C. A. R. *The Future of Socialism.* New York: The Macmillan Company, 1957.

Downs, Anthony. *An Economic Theory of Democracy.* New York: Harper & Row, 1957.

Findlay, J. N. *Values and Intentions.* New York: The Macmillan Company, 1961.

Fried, Albert and Ronald Sanders (eds.). *Socialist Thought A Documentary History.* Garden City, New York: Doubleday & Company, 1964.

Friedman, Milton. *Capitalism and Freedom.* Chicago: University of Chicago Press, 1962.

_____. *Price Theory—A Provisional Text.* Chicago: Aldine Publishing Company, 1962.

Friedrich, Carl and John Chapman (eds.). *Nomos VI Justice.* New York: Atherton Press, 1963.

Galbraith, John Kenneth. *The Affluent Society*. New York: The New American Library, 1958.
_____. *The New Industrial State*. Boston: Houghton Mifflin Company, 1967.
Ginsburg, Morris. *On Justice In Society*. Baltimore: Penguin Books, 1965.
Harrington, Michael. *The Other America*. Baltimore: Penguin Books, 1963.
Hayek, Friedrich. *Individualism and Economic Order*. Chicago: The University of Chicago Press, 1948.
_____. *The Road to Serfdom*. Chicago: The University of Chicago Press, 1944.
Hobhouse, L. T. *The Elements of Social Justice*. New York: Henry Holt and Company, 1922.
Hook, Sidney, ed. *Human Values and Economic Policy*. New York: New York University Press, 1967.
Hume, David. *An Enquiry Concerning the Principles of Morals. Hume's Ethical Writings*. Edited by Alasdair MacIntyre. New York: Collier Books, 1965.
_____. *A Treatise of Human Nature*. Garden City, New York: Doubleday & Company, Inc., 1961.
Jaques, Elliott. *Equitable Payment*. London: Heinemann, 1961.
Jevons, W. Stanley. *The Theory of Political Economy*. Fifth edition. New York: Kelley & Millman Inc., 1957.
Jouvenel, Bertrand de. *The Ethics of Redistribution*. Cambridge: Cambridge University Press, 1952.
Keyserling, Leon. *Progress or Poverty*. Washington, D.C.: Conference on Economic Progress, 1964.
Lerner, Abba. *The Economics of Control*. New York: The Macmillan Company, 1944.
Lippincott, Benjamin E. (ed.). *On the Economic Theory of Socialism*. Minneapolis: The University of Minnesota Press, 1938.
Little, I. M. D. *A Critique of Welfare Economics*. Second edition. Oxford: Clarendon Press, 1957.
Lucas, J. R. *The Principles of Politics*. Oxford: Clarendon Press, 1966.
Lyons, David. *Forms and Limits of Utilitarianism*. Oxford: Clarendon Press, 1965.
Marshall, Alfred. *Principles of Economics*. Eighth edition. New York: The Macmillan Company, 1952.
Marx, Karl. *Critique of the Gotha Program*. London: Lawrence and Wishart Limited, 1938.
_____. *Economic and Philosophic Manuscripts of 1844*. Edited by Dirk J. Struik. Trans. by Martin Millgan. New York: International Publishers, 1964.
_____ and Fredrich Engels. *Selected Works*. 2 vols. Moscow: Foreign Language Publishing House, 1962.
Meade, J. E. *Efficiency, Equality, and the Ownership of Property*. London: George Allen & Unwin Limited, 1964.
Mill, John Stuart. *Mill's Ethical Writings*. Edited by J. B. Schneewind. New York: Collier Books, 1965.
Musgrave, Richard A. *The Theory of Public Finance*. New York: McGraw-Hill Inc., 1959.
Myint, Hla. *Theories of Welfare Economics*. New York: Augustus M. Kelley, 1948.
Narveson, Jan. *Morality and Utility*. Baltimore: The Johns Hopkins Press, 1967.
Perelman, Charles. *The Idea of Justice and the Problem of Argument*. Trans. by John Petrie. New York: The Humanities Press, 1963.
_____. *Justice*. New York: Random House, 1967.
Pigou, Arthur C. *The Economics of Welfare*. Third edition. London: Macmillan and Co. Limited, 1929.
_____. *Wealth and Welfare*. London: Macmillan and Co. Limited, 1912.

Phelps, Edmund J. (ed.). *Private Wants and Public Needs.* Revised edition. New York: W. W. Norton & Company, Inc., 1965.

Quandt, Richard E. and James M. Henderson. *Microeconomic Theory.* New York: McGraw-Hill, 1958.

Reder, M. W. *Studies in the Theory of Welfare Economics.* New York: Columbia University Press, 1947.

Rescher, Nicholas. *Distributive Justice.* New York: The Bobbs Merrill Company, Inc., 1966.

Robbins, Lionel. *An Essay on the Nature and Significance of Economic Science.* Second edition. London: Macmillan and Company, 1935.

———. *Politics and Economics.* London: Macmillan and Company, Lt. D., 1963.

———. *The Theory of Economic Policy in English Classical Political Economy.* London: Macmillan and Company, 1952.

Robertson, D. H. *Utility and All That.* New York: The Macmillan Company, 1952.

Rothenberg, Jerome. *The Measurement of Social Welfare.* Englewood Cliffs, New Jersey: Prentice-Hall Inc., 1961.

Runciman, W. G. *Relative Deprivation and Social Justice.* Berkeley, California: University of California Press, 1966.

Samuelson, Paul. *Economics.* Fifth edition. New York: McGraw-Hill Book Company, Inc., 1961.

———. *Foundations of Economic Analysis.* New York: Atheneum, 1965.

Schumpeter, Joseph A. *Capitalism, Socialism, and Democracy.* Third edition. New York: Harper & Row, 1950.

Scitvosky, Tibor. *Papers on Welfare and Growth.* Stanford: Stanford University Press, 1964.

Shaw, George Bernard (ed.). *Fabian Essays in Socialism.* New York: Humboldt Publishing Company, 1891.

Sidgwick, Henry. *The Elements of Politics.* London: Macmillan and Company, 1891.

———. *The Methods of Ethics.* Seventh edition. Great Britain: The University of Chicago Press, 1962.

———. *Principles of Political Economy.* London: Macmillan & Company, 1883.

Singer, Marcus. *Generalization In Ethics.* New York: Alfred A. Knopf, 1961.

Tawney, R. H. *Equality.* New York: Harcourt Brace and Company, 1929.

Tobin, James. *National Economic Policy.* New Haven: Yale University Press, 1966.

Wicksteed, Philip H. *The Coordination of the Laws of Distribution.* London: The London School of Economics and Political Science, 1932.

Wootton, Barbara. *Freedom Under Planning.* Chapel Hill: The University of North Carolina Press, 1945.

———. *The Social Foundations of Wage Policy.* London: George Allen & Unwin Lt. D., 1955.

Articles

Acton, H. B. and J. W. N. "Symposium: Negative Utilitarianism," *Aristotelian Society Proceedings Supplement* XXXVII (1963), pp. 83–114.

Anderson, John. "Utilitarianism," *Studies in Empirical Philosophy.* Sydney: Angus and Robertson, 1962. Pp. 227–37.

Barone, Enrico. "The Ministry of Production in the Collectivist State," *Collectivist Economic Planning*. Edited by F. A. Hayek. London: Routledge, 1935.

Berlin, Isaiah and Richard Wollheim. "Equality," *Aristotelian Society Proceedings*, LVI (1955-6), pp. 281-326.

Brown, P. M. "Distribution and Values," *Journal of Philosophy*, LXVI (1969), pp. 197-212.

Corkey, R. "Benevolence and Justice," *Philosophical Quarterly*, IX (1959), pp. 152-63.

Emmons, D. C. "Justice Reassessed," *American Philosophical Quarterly*, IV (April, 1967), pp. 144-51.

Ewin, R. E. "On Justice and Injustice," *Mind*, LXXIX (April 1970), pp. 200-16.

Friedman, Milton. "Choice, Chance, and the Personal Distribution of Income," *The Journal of Political Economy*, LXI (1953), pp. 277-92.

――――, and L. J. Savage. "The Utility Analysis of Choices Involving Risk," *The Journal of Political Economy*, LVI (1948), pp. 279-304.

Gaille, W. B. "Liberal Morality and Socialist Morality," *Philosophy, Politics, and Society*. Edited by Peter Laslett. New York: The Macmillan Company, 1956. Pp. 116-33.

Georgescu-Roegen, Nicholas. "Choice, Expectations and Measurability," *Quarterly Journal of Economics*, LXVIII (1954), pp. 503-34.

Hall, Everett M. "Justice as Fairness: A Modernized Version of the Social Contract," *Journal of Philosophy*, LIV (1957), pp. 662-70.

Harsanyi, John C. "Cardinal Welfare, Individualistic Ethics, and Interpersonal Comparisons of Utility," *Journal of Political Economy*, LXI (1955), pp. 309-21.

Hicks, John R. "The Foundations of Welfare Economics," *Economic Journal*, XLIX (1939), pp. 696-712.

Houthakker, H. S. "Revealed Preference and the Utility Function," *Econimica*, n.s. XVII (1950), pp. 159-74.

Kaldor, Nicholas. "Alternative Theories of Distribution," *Review of Economic Studies*, XXIII (1955-6), pp. 83-100.

――――. "Welfare Propositions of Economics and Interpersonal Comparisons of Utility," *The Economic Journal*, XLIX (1939), pp. 549-52.

Lamont, W. D. "Justice: Distributive and Collective," *Philosophy*, XVI (1941), pp. 3-18.

――――, Honor Brotman and J. P. Corbett. "Symposium: The Concept of Welfare In Economics," *Aristotelian Society Proceedings*, Supplement XXVII (1953), pp. 157-223.

Lange, Oscar. "The Determinateness of the Utility Function," *Review of Economic Studies*, I (1934), pp. 218-25.

Leys, Wayne. "Justice and Equality," *Ethics*, LXVII (1956), pp. 17-24.

Lipsey, R. G. and Kelvin Lancaster. "The General Theory of Second Best," *Review of Economic Studies*, XXIV (1956-57), pp. 11-32.

McCloskey, H. J. "Egalitarianism, Equality, and Justice," *Australasian Journal of Philosophy*, XLIV (1966), pp. 50-69.

McNaughton, Robert. "A Metrical Concept of Happiness," *Philosophy and Phenomenological Research*, XIV (September 1953-June 1954), pp. 172-83.

Mitchell, Wesley C. "Bentham's Felicific Calculus," *The Backward Art of Spending Money and Other Essays*. New York: Augustus M. Kelley Inc., 1950. Pp. 177-202.

Raphael, David Daiches. "Equality and Equity," *Philosophy*, XXI (1946), pp. 118-32.

――――. "Justice and Liberty," *Aristotelian Society Proceedings*, LI (1950-1), pp. 167-196.

Rawls, John. "Constitutional Liberty and the Concept of Justice," *Nomos VI Justice*. Edited by Carl Friedrich and John W. Chapman. New York: Atherton Press, 1963. Pp. 98-125.

――――. "Distributive Justice," *Philosophy, Politics, and Society*. Edited by Peter Laslett and W. G. Runciman; third series. New York: Barnes and Noble Inc., 1967. Pp. 58–82.

_____. "Justice as Fairness," *Philosophical Review,* LXVII (1958), pp. 164–94.

_____. "The Sense of Justice," *Philosophical Review,* LXXII (1963), pp. 281–305.

Rescher, Nicholas. "Notes on Preference, Utility, and Cost," *Synthese,* XVI (December, 1966), pp. 332–43.

Sabine, George H. "Justice and Equality," *Ethics,* LXVII (1956), pp. 1–11.

Samuelson, Paul. "Aspects of Public Expenditure Theories," *Review of Economics and Statistics,* XL (1958), pp. 332–6.

_____. "Diagrammatic Exposition of a Theory of Public Expenditure," *Review of Economics and Statistics,* XXXVII (1955), pp. 350–6.

_____. "The Problem of Integrability in Utility Theory," *Economica,* n.s. XVII (1950), pp. 355–85.

_____ "The Pure Theory of Public Expenditure," *Review of Economics and Statistics,* XXXVI (1954), pp. 387–9.

Somerville, John. "Toward A Consistent Definition of Freedom and Its Relation to Value," *Nomos IV Liberty.* Edited by Carl Friedrich. New York: Atherton Press, 1962. Pp. 289–300.

Spiegelberg, Herbert. "A Defense of Human Equality," *The Philosophical Review,* LIII (March, 1944), pp. 101–24.

Stigler, George. "The Development of Utility Theory," 2 Parts. *Journal of Political Economy,* LVIII (1950), pp. 307–27, 373–96.

Tsanoff, Radoslav. "Social Morality and the Principle of Justice," *Ethics,* LXVII (1956), pp. 12–16.

Vickrey, Williams. "Goals of Economic Life: An Exchange of Questions Between Economics and Philosophy," *Goals of Economic Life.* Edited by A. Dudley Ward. New York: Harper & Row, 1953. Pp. 151–76.

Vlastos, Gregory. "Justice," *Revue International de Philosophie,* XI (1957), pp. 324–43.

Williams, Bernard. "The Idea of Equality," *Philosophy, Politics, and Society.* Edited by Peter Laslett and W. G. Runciman. Second series. Oxford: Basil Blackwell, 1962. Pp. 110–131.

Index